HANUMAN
GOD AND EPIC HERO

HANUMAN
GOD AND EPIC HERO

The Origin and Growth of Hanuman in Indian Literary and Folk Tradition

JOGINDER NARULA

MANOHAR
2005

First published 1991
Reprinted 2005

ISBN 81-7304-655-7

Published by
Ajay Kumar Jain *for*
Manohar Publishers & Distributors
4753/23 Ansari Road, Daryaganj
New Delhi 110 002

Typeset by
A J Software Publishing Co. Pvt. Ltd.
New Delhi 110 005

Printed at
Lordson Publishers Pvt. Ltd.
Delhi 110 007

Distributed in South Asia by
FOUNDATION BOOKS
4381/4, Ansari Road
Daryaganj, New Delhi 110 002
and its branches at Mumbai, Hyderabad,
Bangalore, Chennai, Kolkata

For My Mother
Surast

Preface

This book is the outcome of my Delhi University doctoral thesis on Sanskrit literature on Hanuman in Sanskrit drama, having undergone major changes in style and content. God Hanuman has an important place in present day India and is worshipped regularly by millions of people. However, an analysis of this phenomenon of God Hanuman has been relegated to only a few pages in scholarly works on Indian gods.

This study contributes to the understanding of a god who is the archetype of honesty, loyalty and courage. Hanuman, perhaps more than any other folk god, is endowed with human qualities cherished by the Kshatriya and Rajput traditions of India. In the book, for the Sanskrit name Hanumana the popular spelling Hanuman is adopted.

I would like to thank DR. Satnam Duggal of Delhi University for directing me to the study of Hanuman for my doctoral thesis. I have also learnt much from my post-graduate work at Centre for Religious Studies, University of Toronto. I would also like to acknowledge my gratitude to Bhupinder and Inder Jandoo for making my stay in Toronto both pleasant and fruitful.

CONTENTS

INTRODUCTION

Hanuman is well known throughout rural and urban India. He is the hero of many folk stories and a popular subject of village plays and dances. His likenesses in stone and wood adore many shrines. His brightly coloured pictures are sold in city streets and hung on the walls of homes and shops.

Shrines of Hanuman are found beneath *pipal* trees on stone or brick platforms specially constructed to support the image, near cremation grounds and in busy market squares, usually under a tree. His figure often appears in the shrines of Rama and Sita where he is usually represented as a monkey lying at their feet with his tail around them. As a roughly hewn red monkey, he is also installed near shrines of Siva. In the countryside, the shrines dedicated to Hanuman outnumber those dedicated to Rama and Sita. Many of them are located in north India but villages and towns of south India also have significant numbers.

In front of Hanuman's image are placed flowers, fruits and other offerings. In North India a sweet called *rot*[1] is considered the specail food of Hanuman.

Hanuman's image is painted *ingur* (vermillion) or *sindur* (red ochre). Tuesday and Saturday are special days for his worship when his image is rubbed with oil and sindur. Both oil and red colour are siad to be pleasing to him. Local folklore states that Sita, pleased with Hanuman, offered him a rosary of pearls. The rosary being without the name of Rama on it, Hanuman felt disappointed. Sensing this Sita, removed some sindur from her forehead and gave it to Hanuman and said, "This *sindur* is the symbol of my good fortune and luck, it is more precious to me than anything else in this world." [2]It is for this reason, the legend asserts, that Hanuman is rubbed with *sindur*.

K.C. Aryan mentions another folk interpretation of the use of *sindur* on Hanuman's image. Once Hanuman was severely wounded in a fierce battle. The only thing that could heal his wound was the application of *sindur* mixed with ghee.[3] In the folk medicine of India, *sindur* is reputed for its healing properties and is regarded as an effective cure for wounds, cuts and burns. In K.C. Aryan's view, the image of Hanuman annointed with *sindur* symbolises his heroic and *Karamvira* (man of action) aspects.[4]

Hanuman in his iconographic representations has a monkey face , a human body and a long tail. He is usually shown flying towards the south. His right foot is in an uplifted position, as if in motion and underneath it is a crushed demon. He holds a mace in his right hand a mounatin in his left. On festival days he is clothed and decorated with earrings, necklaces, bracelets and other ornaments. His statue is smeared afresh with *sindur* as form of worship and devotion.

By the late medieval period, Hanuman was established as a *brahmacari* (celibate). Women in some regions of India avoid touching him. He is also the god of wrestlers and before engaging in wrestling bouts, wrestlers invoke his name for inspiration.

Like other Hindu deities, Hanuman has many names signifying divine and human attributes. Some of his names are Mahavira, Mahabali, Bajrang-bali, Samkata Mocana, Anjanisuta, Pavanputra, Rudrarupa, Rudravatara, Maruti and Anilatmaja. He is usually worshipped as a protector deity and the reliever of evil who keeps away ghosts and spirits. His birthday is celebrated in several parts of India with great enthusiasm . Hanuman's birthday is celebrated on the 15th day of the Hindu lunar month of Chaitra.

That Hanuman is linked with Visnu through his devotion to Rama is not surprising. Rama is an incarnation of Visnu. The Sri among the Vaisnavas worship Garuda and Hanuman alike as the mount of Visnu. In the 16th century Bangiya Vaisnava scripture of *Astavimsati*, Hanuman is worshipped in various forms as *angadevta.*[5] The Tantrikas worship one-headed, five-headed and eleven-headed Hanumans to attain spiritual attainment. The Tantrika texts *Narada Purana* and *Sudarshan Chakraraj Samhita* contain elaborate descriptions of various forms of Hanuman worship.[6] Hanuman worship in association with yoni worship in Tantra is worth investigation. Hanuman is generally considered a celibate god.

There is no scholarly work in English on Hanuman that utilises Indian literature in Sanskrit to delineate his importance as a god and confident of Rama. Although Hanuman is a popular folk god in India, he has not received attention commensurate with this popularity, from either Indian or Western scholars of religion and mythology. However Hanuman's iconographical development as a god has received attention from Govinda Chandra Rai,[7] G.S.Ghurye,[8] J.N.Banerjee[9] and K.C. Aryan.[10] A historical survey of iconography of Hanuman and his evolution as a folk-god has been undertaken by Govinda Chandra Rai. Camile Bulcke has outlined some of the myths and texts concerning Hanuman.[11] Walcott has written on

Hanuman's religious significance in the various beliefs and practices in the folk religion of the Bhojpuri language speaking area of east U.P. and Bihar. Because he lacks the mythological richness and iconographic sophistication of other major Hindu gods such as Siva or Visnu, Hanuman is ignored in major studies of Hindu gods. As a god, Hanuman is too mundane. He is regarded as an earthly god concerned with success and material well-being. For scholars primarily concerned with mysticism and spirituality he is of little interest, for he does not seem to embody other worldliness. He is rarely assigned philosophical attributes as in the *Madhva Sampradaya* where he is represented as *paramjnana*, the god of of ultimate knowledge. He lacks the sensuous appeal of god Krsna. He rather has an ascetic streak for he is a lifelong celibate.

Hanuman makes his initial appearance in the Hindu pantheon during the Puranic period (4th to 9th centuries A.D.). He is considered to be a derivative of Vedic deity Marut (wind god) and is associated with Indra and Vrsakapi.[13] His zoomorphic form suggests that he was originally a god of lower classes or aboriginal communities (possibly of non-Aryan origin), later incorporated into the Brahmanic tradition.[14]

There is however a wide-ranging scholarly debate on whether Hanuman is a monkey or a human.[16] The *Ramayana* of Valmiki and the Sanskrit play portray Hanuman as a monkey with human, superhuman and godly attributes. However, in modern India he is regarded as a god.

This study explores the human and superhuman role of Hanuman in Sanskrit texts. With the *Ramayana* and its critical editions as the basic sources, Sanskrit plays and *Puranas* have also been studied to unravel the complexity of Hanuman's personality and its development as a character in flesh and blood. Hanuman is also analysed in the context of religious tradition centred on Ramayana.The study focusses on the evolution and change in the theology of Hanuman. Hanuman appears as an incarnation of Siva, a god in his own right, a tribal deity and a hero god with power and virility who destroys evil. At a mundane level, Hanuman is an ideal human, an upright man, a trusted friend of Rama, a statesman and a brave warrior. In the *bhakti* (relegious devotion) tradition he is the lord, the object of *bhakti*.

PART ONE

I THE ORIGIN OF HANUMAN

Hanuman in the Ramayana

Hanuman's mysterious origin and his superhuman activities are described in the Ramayana and the *Puranas*. The reason why Hanuman acquired his name is stated in the *Yuddha Kanda* of the *Ramayana* Hanuman had the body of a *vajra* (thunderbolt) and the speed of a Garuda. In his childhood, he leapt towards the sky to catch the sun, mistaking it for a fruit. He could not reach the sun, and fell down on the mountain Udayagiri and cut his chin. Thus, having his chin cut in so peculiarly a manner, he came to be known as Hanuman, the one who possesses a typical chin.[1]

Sage Agastya in the *Uttara Kanda* recounts the story with a little variation. Hanuman in the absence of his mother Anjana, felt hungry and leapt towards the sun and caught hold of it. Being the day of a solar eclipse, Rahu also had come to grab the sun. Finding the sun in the grip of Hanuman, Rahu went to Indra. Acting on his complaint, Indra struck Hanuman with his thunderbolt. Hanuman fell to the mountain and broke his chin. Finding his son injured, the grieving wind god stopped functioning. The worried Brahma along with Indra and others called on the wind god and requested him to relent. Brahma revived Hanuman and conferred various boons on him. Indra blessed him and prophesied that "he will become famous as Hanuman and in future his *vajra* (thunderbolt) will do no harm to him".[2]

In both the above stories, Hanuman's ability to fly at will is emphasized. His obsession with the Sun, the source of natural power, is significant. However, Hanuman, considered to be a minor god, cannot match the power of Indra and other gods, and gets his chin broken whin he tries to compete with them. He is thus given a lower status in the Ramayana vis-a-vis other other gods such as Indra and Brahma. Significantly, this story identifies him as the son of Vayu, the wind god.

Hanuman as Vayuputra

Hanuman's relationship with Vayu is reflected in the refrences to and the modes of address used for him in the *Ramayana.* He is called Pavanaputra, Vayputra, Maruti (son of Marut), Vayusunu, Samirasunu, Anilatmaja, etc. Hanuman is described as the son of Vayu, born out of the latter's union with Anjana but out of wedlock. *Kiskindha Kanda* explicitly states this fact in Hanuman's birth story. A cursed Apsara named Punjikasthala took birth as a *vanari.* She became the wife of Kesari and daughter of Kunjara. Being a *kamarupni,* she could assume any form one day, she transformed into a beautiful woman and was strolling over a hill when Vayu saw her and charmed by her beauty, embraced her. Her feeble protests vanished when Vayu promised her a son as valiant, intelligent and swift as himself. Anjana thus conceived Hanuman.[3] The godly origin of Hanuman is thus emphasised. Hanuman is, therefore, both a *vanara* and son of a god.

According to Luders, the name Vayuputra is used in sense of a *vidyadhara* (magician).[4] In *Sumaga Jataka,* for instance, a *vidyadhara* is called a *vayuputra.*[5] One of the attributes of *vidyadhara* is that they can fly at will. Rai argues that Hanuman, before being incorporated as character in the *Ramayana* was probably a yaksa.[6] Yaksa are also known for performing supernatural feats such as flying jumping etc. Bulcke too is of the opinion that the term Vayuputra as an epithet to Hanuman, was popular before the composition of the *Ramayana.*[7]

Origin of Hanuman in Jaina Literature

The Jaina *Ramayana* is an adaptation of Valmiki *Ramayana* with major thematic changes. The two main works on Rama are by Vimalasuri and Gunabhadra.[8] They differ form each other on many points. The story of Hanuman's birth is narrated in the *Paumacariyam* (c. 200-400 A.D.) of Vimalasuri. Prince Pavanajaya of Aditypura married Anjana, the Princess of Mahendrapura. Before his marriage with Anjana, he overheard some insulting remarks about himself being made by her. He took remarks seriously and wanting to take revenge, remained sexually indifferent to her for twenty two years. Once he went to battlefield to support Ravana against Varuna. There one evening he suddenly felt enamoured of his wife and proceeded to Aditypura and secretly consummated the marraige. Anjana became pregnant. Accusing her of infidelity, her parents-in-law turned her out along with a friend Vasantamala. Even her parents did not accept her. She gave birth to a son in a cave. Her maternal uncle Pratisurya took her to Hunuruhapura along with her son. On their way to Hunuruhapura, the child jumped form his mother's lap and fellon a rock. She alighted from the vimana and found that the rock had been completely smashed into pieces while the boy was smiling and sucking his toe. After coming from the battlefield, Pavanajaya disclosed the truth and she was again declared a chaste woman. Anjana was then taken back to her parents-in-law along with her son. Owing to her stay in Hunuruhapura, the child was named Hanuman.[9] Hanuman's supernatural strength manifested at his birth is abundantly highlighted in the story. Also keeping with the mystery surrounding his birth, his birth is at first tainted with illegitimacy. Hanuman's birth and his adventures, therefore, have a dash of supernatural.

The story in the *Uttara Purana* (c. 800-900 A.D.) of Gunabhadra is dramatically different form Vimalasuri and also further away form Valmiki. Prabhanjana *vidyadhara* was the king of Vidyut Kanta. He had a son named Amitteja. One day, Amitteja, keeping his right foot on a mountain, kicked the Sun with his other foot. Since he assumed a very tiny form he was called Anuman. From Anuman he became Hanuman.[10]

The *Padam Purana* (c. 500-800 A.D.) by Ravisenacarya states that Hanuman was named Sri Saila by his uncle because the rock that he fell upon was smashed to pieces. Later he was named Hanuman after the name of the city Hanuruhangar whrere he was brought up.[11]

A similiar story about Hanuman's birth is given in the Jaina play *Anjana Pavanajaya Nataka* (c. 1300 A.D.) with a few variations. Whereas the *Paumacariyam* refers to the indifference of Pavanajaya towards his wife for twenty-two years, this drama does not mention it at all. According to this drama, Anjana married Pavanajaya through a *svayamvara* (choosing a groom by one's own choice).[12] The child is brought up in Anuruhadvipas. The city that Hanuman is named after is, not mentioned.

In Jaina literature, Hanuman, Sugriva and the other vanaras are not represented as animals having long tails and displaying beastly behaviour. These *vanaras* are depicted as *vidyadharas* or a class of beings endowed with many human and supernatural qualities.The Jaina representation of them is of people who got their names because of the custom of wearing the symbol of a monkey on their crowns and flags.[13]

Puranas

The Puranic myths indicate Hanuman's close association with Siva,

Rudra and Vayu. These myths associate Hanuman's power with Siva's power and his benevolent and malevolent forms. In early Puranic texts,[14] Hanuman is called the amsa of Siva and later, an incarnation of Siva, but he is not recognised as an independent deity. The sectarian *Siva Puranas* even suggest that Hanuman got his power from Siva to fulfill Rama's task.

Hanuman and the Wind God

According to the *Narsimha Purana* (c. 400-500 A.D.), all *vanaras* are born from the *amsa* of gods to eliminate Ravana. Hanuman is the son of the wind god.[15]

In the *Visnudharmotra Purana* (c. 500-700 A.D.), all the *vanaras* are born from *devyoni* (divine womb). Bali is born from Indra, Nila from Agni, Nala from Visvakarma and Hanuman from Vayu. They are brave, strong and know the *dharma-shastra* and politics.[16]

The *Skanda Purana* (c. 800-900 A.D.) mentions that Anjana, the wife of Kesari was issueless. On the advice of *rsis*, she fasted and did penance for twelve years. The wind god was pleased and blessed that he would take birth as her son.[17] The son was named Hanuman. In the *Avanti Khanda* of the *Skanda Purana* , Hanuman is mentioned as Rudravatara.[18]

Hanuman and Siva

In the *Bhavisya Purana* (c. 700 A.D.), Kesari is designated as the father of Hanuman, but Rudra and Vayu also shared in his birth. Ravana became a menace on earth. The scared gods worshipped Siva for eleven years to secure his help in protecting themselves. Siva promised them that he would take birth as an incarnation to destroy Ravana. Siva as Rudra entered the moutn of Kesari and he (Kesari) in turn had sex with Anjana (daughter of Gautama). Vayu too entered the body of Kesariand had sex with Anjana.[19] After twelve years Anjana became pregnant and gave birth to a son who had the face of a *vanara*. Finding her son ugly faced, Anjana threw him away. After his birth, Hanuman seized the sun. He was hurt severally by Indra's thunderbolt but even then he did not release the sun. Hearing the cries of the sun. Ravana came to his rescue and pulled Hanuman's tail. After much struggle, Hanuman left the sun and started fighting with Ravana. The fight between the two went on for a year. Ravana was defeated but Hanuman continued to strike him. The sage Visrava then pacified the *Rudravatra* Hanuman and rescued Ravana from his grip.[20] Like in the *Ramayana*, the birth of Hanuman is directly related to the gods in *Puranas*. The gods, through dubious ways, are responsible for his birth. Hanuman's tryst with the sun god is also found in other Puranic versions. Although the Puranic stories are slightly different, they are closer to the *Ramayana* in so far as they mention the illegitimacy of Hanuman and his dealings with the sun god. The fight with Ravana and his defeat by Hanuman is a new feature introduced in the Puranas.

In the *Brahmavaivarta Purana* (c. 800 A.D., recast in the present form in c. 1600 A.D.), Hanuman is said to be born form the *amsa* of Siva.[21] Siva took birth as the son of Vayu, as has been mentioned in the *Mahabhagavata Purana* (c.1000-1100 A.D.).[22] The *Brddharma Purana* (c.1300 A.D.) also mentions that Hanuman is the incarnation of Siva.[23] It states that Hanuman advises Devi Lanka to leave Lanka because Sita has been insulted by Ravana. Devi Lanka calls Hanuman *saksatadeva mahesvaram* (the true manifestation of god).[24]

The *Siva Maha Purana* (c.1300-1400 A.D.) refers to Hanuman as the *amsa* of Siva born to accomplish Rama's mission.[25] He is called an incarnation of Rudra and Siva . Besides this name, he is assigned various other names too.[26] Once Visnu assumed the form of a beautiful damsel. Siva, aroused by her beauty discharged semen. The seven *rsis* kept the semen in a leaf and poured into the ears of Anjana. In due course , Siva was born to her in the form of a monkey named Hanuman.[27]

The story of the *Siva Maha Purana* is echoed in Hanuman legends orally transmitted by the *adivasis* (tribals) of North and Central India. In the Baiga tribe of central India, Hanuman is beleived to have been born of Kariandani, in whose ears the *virya* (semen) of Mahadev (Siva) was poured.[28]

This striking resemblence between the tribal legends and Puranic myths raises the important issues of interaction between *Purana* stories and local folk legends. It is likely that the *Siva Maha Purana* (which is in Sanskrit and not known to the tribals) encompasses the local legends ,giving them a sectarian tinge.

According to the *Siva Purana*, Nandi existed in the form of Hanuman to accomplish the task of Rama.[29] Hanuman is thus described as Nandi, one of the prominent *ganas* (attendants) of Siva. The *Visnudharmotra Purana* (c. 500 A.D.) states that

Ravana , travelling in his Pushpaka *vimana*, faced a barrier and slowed as he approached the Kailash mountain. He looked around and found Nandi on the top of the mountain in the shape of a *vanara*. Ravana laughed at him. Annoyed, Nandi cursed him and said that a *vanara* with a face like him would take birth and destroy him. Since Ravana was a devotee of Siva and worshipped his ten forms, he could not destroy his ten forms. Siva, therefore, assumed the eleventh form of a *vanara* with the intention of helping Rama crush Ravana, the evil on earth.

In the *Narada Purana* (c. 900-1000 A.D.), Hanuman has been called Trambaka Sambhava and Sarvajana, encompassing Visnu, Brahma and Siva.[31]

Hanuman and Vrsakapi

The *Brahma Purana* (c. 1000-1300 A.D.) does not mention Hanuman as Rudra or Siva. Here Hanuman is associated with Vrsakapi. Kesari with his two wives was living on the Anjana parvata (mountain). Both the wives were celestial nymphs. Due to the curse of Indra they took birth as human beings. One was Anjana with the face of a *vanara* and the other became cat-faced and was called as Adrika. Once, in the absence of their husband Kesari, they warmly welcomed *rsi* Agastya and begged him to grant them a boon so that they would have strong and noble sons. Granting the boon to them, *rsi* Agastya left the place. One day, when Adrika and Anjana were strolling on the mountain, Vayu and Nrti saw them and had sex with them. Soon, Hanuman was born of Vayu and Anjana; Adrika and Nrti gave birth to Adri who later became the king of pisacas.[32] Adri took Anjana to a pilgrimage site on the river Gotami (Godavari). There she took a bath, was freed from the curse of Indra and assumed her original form as an Apsara. The site is, therefore, named Anjana or Pisacam. Hanuman took Adrika to some another sacred spot near Gotami. She too was freed of the curse by taking a bath and went to heaven. This spot is named Vrsakapi.[33]

The *Brahma Purana* states that the confluence of *Phena* and *Gotami* (Godawari) is popularly known as Hanuman and Vrsakapi.[34]

Most of the *Puranas* which mention Hanuman and his birth are Saivite *Puranas*. Hanuman's close association with Rudra, Siva and Nandi Siva's *vahana* (vehicle), is emphasized in these sectarian *Puranas*. According to them, Hanuman is either an *amsa* or the son of Siva but Siva is not his legal father, i.e., he is not born of Siva's wives. In the *Puranas*, the role of Vayu as the father of Hanuman is explained away by stating that Vayu is an avtar of Siva. The miraculous heroic qualities of Hanuman mentioned in these *Puranas* are in line with those attributed to him in the *Ramayana*. The *Puranic* myths of Hanuman's birth, as in the *Ramayana*, are closely linked with gods. The *Siva Puranas*, using the Ramayana as their source, evidently have absorbed Hanuman within the sectarian fold.

Later Rama Kathas

The semi-divine birth of Hanuman also preoccupies the mind of the author of *Ananda Ramayana* (c. 1400-1500 A.D.). The Apsara, Suvarcala, was an expert dancer. Owing to an imperfect dancing performance,an angry Brahma cursed her that she would become a *patanga* (kite). However, she was also granted a boon that she would assume her previous form if she were to drop *payasa* (milk rice) on the Anjani mountain. When an oppurtunity came, she snatched *payasa* of Kaikeyi's hands and dropped on the mountain. Hanuman was thus born on the Anjani mountain. Suvarcala regained her original form and went to the heavenly world.[35]

Hanuman's miraculous birth is emphasized here. The *payasa* is obviously a substitute for semen and Anjana is metamorphosed into a female mountain. An Apsara, a semi-divine being, becomes the instrument of a union between *payasa* and the Anjana mountain. Hanuman's birth in this myth is almost miraculous, i.e., without a physical human or supernatural sexual union.

However, in another *sarga* of the *Ananda Ramayana*, we find a combination of both the miraculous and physical elements in the birth. The *payasa*, dropped from the mounth of the *patanga* which is actually a heavenly Apsara, is eaten by Anjana the wife of Kesari. After partaking of the *payasa*, Anjana has a union with the wind god Vayu and gives birth to Hanuman.[36]

Hanuman is identified in the *Ananda Ramayana* as a folk god on earth. Sita blesses Hanuman and prophesies that he will be worshipped in villages and cities under the *pipal* trees and will be known for his power of preventing calamities.[37] Rama gives a talisman, known as Hanuman kavaca (shield of Hanuman), to Vibhisana to help him ward off ghosts,evil spirits and protect him from fever.[38] Without referring to Hanuman, Garuda in the *Ananda Ramayana*, explains the monkey worship to Rama. He say that this should be done during *mahamari* (malaria epidemic).[39] That there is a close association between Hanuman and Rudra-Siva worship is clear in the *Ananda Ramayana*. In another instance, he is designated as a *Saksata Rudra* (true).[40] When Hanuman sets up a *sivalinga* in *setubandha* (Rameshwaram) Rama pledges to Hanuman that whoever goes to Rameshwaram without worshipping *sivalinga* (set up by Hanuman) would not get any reward even if he worshipped other gods.[41] Interestingly, Hanuman, at Rameshwaram, is a folk god which must be paid homage along with Siva. It is also noteworthy that it is from setubandha that Hanuman flew to Lanka according to *Valmiki Ramayana.*

Drama

The playwright Hastimalla in his *Anjana Pavanajaya Nataka* (c. 1300 A.D.) states that Anjana gave birth to Hanuman in the Matangmalini forest where she had to undergo many trials and tribulations in the course of her wanderings. Soon after attempting to grab the Sun, the infant Hanuman fell on the rock. He sustained no injury but the rock into pieces.[42]

In the *Anargha Raghava Nataka* (c. 900-1000 A.D.), Hanuman is brave and strong but is unaware of his strength due to the curse of Brahma.[43] The dramas, mostly written during the medieval period, merely repeat Hanuman's birth stories readily available in the *Ramayana* and the *Puranas.* Hanuman is recognised in the dramas as a son of Vayu. However, the epithet Kesariputra, son of Kesari is rarely used for him. In some plays, he is called Anjanisuta or Anjaneya, thereby linking his parentage to Anjani. In the 20th-century play *Prasanna Hanuman Nataka,* the father is explicitly recognised as Kesari. According to that play, Kesari received a boon that he would have a son like him and Hanuman was born subsequently. In the *Ramayana* and the *Puranas,* Hanuman's parentage is semi-divine and illegitimate. The 20th-century version, with its new sense of family virtue, emphasises Hanuman's birth as a result of a legitimate union between a husband and wife.

Hanuman's association with the Saivite sect is taken for granted in some of the plays. In the *Hanuman Nataka* (c. 1000-1400 A.D.), it is stated that Ravana, finding his city completely destroyed is convinced that it is the work of Hanuman, the manifestation of Rudra.[44] Jambavana advises Rama to propitiate the Rudravatara Hanuman in order to accomplish his task.[45]

II HANUMAN AS *CIRANJIVA* (IMMORTAL)

Hanuman's immortality is evidently due to his semi-divine birth. He is born out of a union between a fallen Apsara and the wind god in one case and in the other he is the result of Siva's virya. Besides narrating the semi-divine origin of Hanuman, the Valmiki Ramayana refers to the boon of immotality given by the god Indra to him that he would not die unless he wished so.[1] At the end of the Ramayana, Rama too gives a boon of immortality to Hanuman.[2] Presumably this is the origin of Hanuman's immortality expounded by later dramatists and Rama Katha (story) writers. For instance, the *Adhyatama Ramayana* mentions the same boon given to Hanuman as found in the *Ramayana*.[3] In the *Hanuman Nataka* and the *Prasanna Hanuman Nataka*, Hanuman is bestowed with the boon of immortality along with Vibisana.[4] That Hanuman's immortality has been established much before the writing of the drama, is obvious from the *Mahabharata*. At the end of the war, Sita blesses Hanuman with the boon of immortality.[5]

Hanuman's immortality was easier to establish in his Puranic stories because of his blood kinship with a god. In the Saivite *Skanda Purana*, it is stated that Hanuman fell unconscious when Indra struck him with his *vajra*. His father, the wind god, prayed for Siva's help and worshipped the *Sivalinga* in the *Mahakara Vana*. Hanuman recovered at the touch of the *linga*. Siva then conferred on Hanuman the boon of immortality.[6]

According to the *Visnudharmotra Purana*, the sun and other gods, in order to please the wind god granted Hanuman the boon of immortality .[7] He is considered one of the seven immortals and worshipped on sacred occasions along with other *rsis*.[8]

Hanuman thus owes his immortality not only to the blessings of Rama and other gods but also to the fact of his being the son of Vayu, the wind (the most important of five elements) god. Without Vayu, there cannot be any life. Vayu is all pervasive, omnipotent and immortal.[9] Hanuman, being the son of wind, is also immortal, all powerful and omnipresent.

III ARYAN AND DRAVIDIAN ORIGINS OF HANUMAN

The reference to Vrsakapi in the dialogue of Indra and Indrani in a Rgvedic hymn[1] has led to a debate among scholars regarding the position of Vrsakapi in Rgvedic society. The Vrsakapi hymn indicates, according to Velankar, that Vrsakapi, perhaps a dasa chief, was held in certain quarters of the Vedic society, in greater esteem than Indra.[2] However, according to Velankar, reference to Vrsakapi is made only once in the *Rgveda*. Pargitar, while arguing that the cult of Vrsakapi may not have been anti Indra as the reference in the Rgveda might suggest, feels that it was a powerful non-Aryan monkey cult which had to be assimilated by the Vedic Aryans.[3] The reference to Vrsakapi thus alludes to the importance given to the monkey god in Vedic times. Pargitar refers to the story of Vrsakapi as related in the *Brahma Purana* where he is closely associated with Hanuman.[4] The *Brahma Purana* (ch. 84) elaborates the importance of pilgrimage of

Vrsakapi and Hanumant, the pilgrimage centres at the confluence of the Godavari and Phena rivers.[5] Vrsakapi and Hanumant are thus inextricably linked at the time of the composition of the *Brahma Purana*, according to Pargitar.

Pargiatr's linguistic analysis of the terms Vrsakapi and Hanumant merits serious cosideration. He states that Vrsakapi consists of two words which mean male monkey.[6] The Tamil and Malayalam equivalent of Vrsakapi is Anmandi which in turn became Hanumant in its Sanskritised form.[7] According to Rai, *vrsa* is joined with *kapi* because the word stands for a male monkey who is a strong *vrsa* (bull).[8] Again according to Pargitar Hanuman's was originally a non-Aryan cult which was later absorbed in the Aryan religion.[9] S.K.Chatterji supports Pargitar's contension that Hanuman was of Dravidian origin and states that he was "a great monkey god, eventuallu adopted by the Aryans and remains still a powerful deity popular in Hinduism, the sublimation of his character by *bhakti* adding fresh lustre to his pristime popularity as a strong helper in need and remover of distress, the rough and ready god of primitive people."[10]

Thus linguistic and historical research attest the Dravidian and non-Aryan nature of the folk god Hanuman, whose monkeyhood and earthliness are of great antiquity. It is noteworthy that the Hanuman of the *Valmiki Ramayana* is encountered by Rama as soon as he crosses Dandakaranya to the South.

G.S.Ghurye observes that Hanuman, representing in Brahmanical culture the zoomorphic Vrsakapi of the Rgvedic era, has come to acquire a special signifiance of his own as he has been kept out of the complex of deities formulated in the syncretic era of Brahmanism.[11] However, Ghurye postulates a basic transforamtion of the vedic Vrsakapi into Hanuman. He states, " In Panini's times Vrsakapi was beleived to have a consort; for Panini derives the word Vrsakapayi, the wife of Vrsakapi. But Hanuman is one of the permanently young *brahmacaris* of the Hindu mythology."[12]

IV HANUMAN AS YAKSA

As a folk god not fully assimilated in the Brahmanic pantheon of great gods, Hanuman resembles the ubiquitous yaksas of Indian literature. Hanuman, like the yaksas, can assume any form. The yaksas are associated with fertility cults. Women worship Hanuman in North India to have children. The yaksas are called immortal. Hanuman, having received the boon of immortality is also called immortal. The epithet Vira is used to refer to the yaksas. One of Hanuman's titles is Mahavira. The yaksas are keepers of wealth, guardians, protectors and wardens of villages and towns. Aggarwala alluding to the two forms by which Hanuman is presently worshipped states that onc is a clearly delineated and carved image form while the other is made of lumps of clay the yaksas' image. [1] He further states that like the yaksas Hanuman is offered a *puja* of water, red cloth and *rakt chandan dhoopmala*. However, no animal is sacrificed in his worship. His flag is coloured red. He is associated with eating *pan* (which results in red spittle). Like the yaksas he is smeared with *sindur* which is often linked with the worship of true godlings.[2] Aggarwal adds that Hanuman's *samkata mokana* (destroyer of calamities) role is similar to yaksas' worship. His names, Maruti, Mahavira and Bajrangbali resemble yaksas' names. Hanuman is one of the *panca mahabhuta* (the five local godlings) whose worship, like that of the yaksas, brings immediate results.[3]

Hanuman is not identified anywhere as a yaksa. However, assuming that the term yaksa is a generic term for local gods, Hanuman surely fits in that category. J.N. Banerjee refers to the fact that the yaksas in ancient Indian literature are known to assume animal forms.[4] In the *Mahabharata*, *Maccha* yaksa is in the form of the fish. An elephant face yaksa appears in Amravati sculpture.[5] Image of yaksas according to Coomaraswami and Banerjee, were placed under trees and shrines built round them.[6] The worship of spirits and gods who live in trees is a common phenomenon in the villages of India today. Tree and yaksa worship has been authenticated in ancient Indian literature too. Hanuman is thus a part of the local folk culture. He is one of the folk gods who along with a host of other yaksas and spirits, are regularly worshipped in several regions of India.[7]

Valmiki perhaps chose the local folk- god (*yaksa*) Hanuman for his epic Rama story. In Indian literature however, the association of Vrsakapi with Hanuman throws light on the earlier Vedic, non-Aryan origin of monkey worship.

The worship of the monkey Kapi as a god is found among many tribes of India. The Bhuyia tribe of Keonjhar worship Kapi as Vira and Mahavira. The Bhuyia tribe of Singbhum consider Kapi to be the son of Pavan and worship him. The fishermen of East Bengal worship Kapi as deity.[8] The Bheels worship Hanuman with the belief that he is an extraordinary Vira and magician.[9]

Kapi worship, the yaksa and tree, spirit and Hanuman worship thus are different manifestations of a belief in a folk god. The similarities between yaksas and Hanuman, the modes worship recommended and followed by their devotees in both ancient and modern times reinforce the folk god origin of Hanuman. It is important to note that there are folk gods in Maharashtra who are simply referred to as *viroba* (*vira* is a hero and *ba* is an honorific suffix). In Uttar Pradesh too there are Mahavira and Vira cults which are not specifically affiliated to Hanuman worship.[10]

V HANUMAN WORSHIP AND HIS ATTRIBUTES IN MODERN INDIA

As stated in the *Ananda Ramayana* Hanuman is recognised as a protector god who wards off evils and other calamities in actual practice today. *Mantras* (formulae) in his praise are repeated at the beginning of each day and before starting any important work. A small pamphlet called *Hanuman Calisa*, forty verses about Hanuman abstracted from the *Ramayana*, is used for incantation. It also acts as a talisman. The name Hanuman Mahavira (the brave one) is recited to excise demons and gain mastery over one's enemies. The most frequently used epithet to Hanuman by the villagers is Mahavira or Mahavirji (The Brave One).The salutations given to him are *Jai Bajrang Bali, Jai Mahavira, Jai Hanuman* (Victory be Hanuman's, Hail Mahavira). Folk songs and hymns in praise of Hanuman addressing him as the son of Anjana and devotee of Rama. The songs recount his childhood adventures of grabbing the sun. They narrate how Hanuman overcame great dangers with courage and intelligence.

Wolcott observes that Hanuman is a particularly favourite god among men. Many men wear a crested medallion bearing his figure around their necks as a talisman. Men regale themselves by telling stories about Hanuman's extraordinary strength.[1] Manohar Sharma states that in Rajasthan folktales, men and women have separate songs on Hanuman and each group takes care not to repeat the other's songs.[2]

Judging from the depiction of Hanuman in the *Ramayana* and the *Puranas* as a hero of great prowess, it is natural that he is regarded as the patron god of wrestlers in several of India. In Ranchi, during events involving the traditional Indian sports of bowmanship, swordsmanship, stick fighting and wrestling, Hanuman's grace is sought eagerly by invoking his name. The participants in such events almost always start their game by saluting Hanuman, viz., Mahavirji, jai Bajrang Bali, Langote wale ki jai.[3] Every akhada (wrestlers' arena) in Maharashtra keeps a picture of Hanuman as its patron god.[4]

In the *Tulsidas Ramayana*, Hanuman's *sakti* (power) comes from Rama, whose name and remembrance give power and protection. Tulsidas says that before commencing any exploits, Hanuman seeks sterngth through devotion to Rama. In the combat with Ravana, Hanuman receives his *sakti* by such means.[5] In folk literature, however, Hanuman is the embodiment of *sakti*, although he derives his *sakti* from being an incarnation of Siva or Rudra. It is significant, therefore, that his shrine is often attached or forms a part of a Siva temple. The spells and incantations which invoke Hanuman's *sakti* to prevail upon demonic spirits sometimes contain references to Rama and Laksmana but more often they incorporate Siva and Parvati. Wolcott emphasises the *sakti* aspect of Hanuman worship and says "by virtue of his strength and virility, he is the immediate representation of power to exist."[6] For the Bhojpuri speaking men, according to Wolcott, "strength of limb, and body's virility are dependent on Hanuman Puja." Hanuman "is an accessible and comprehensible embodiment of the power in its most familiar form, as bodily strength."[7] Hanuman worship is thus geared towards immediate fulfillment of material objectives and wishes. He is not worshipped for attainment of *Moksa* (salvation).

Hanuman is worshipped by women and given a place of honour in Central and North India. In the Bundeli tales, women consider him an *Istadevata* (one's chosen diety), living in heaven. They send invitations to him by climbing on a *pat* (stand). They feel that by doing so, the invitations will reach him without obstructions. They worship him as a child god too. Affectionately, they address him as langur.[8] In Bhojpuri and North Indian folk tales, Hanuman is worshipped by women to achieve pregnancy and cure barrenness.[9]

The various epithets to Hanuman represent different facets of his *sakti* (power). The *Langola Upanisada*, a collection of Hanuman *mantras*, describes him as the eleventh incarnation of Rudra and a *kumar brahmacari*.[10] In the *Sri Hanumat Sahastranama Stotra*, he is called *Garbhadosadhana* and *Putrapautroda*. As a *samkata mocana* god, he is called appropriately, *samsarbhya nasaka, Saranagate vatsala, Bhagawana, Jagannatha, Anadi* etc.[11] Hanuman is also regarded as a great leader. Rai mentions an undated manuscript *Kapindra Prayaga* which recommends certain prayers for relieving bodily pains.[12] In the *Rudramal Tantra*, use of Hanuman oil is recommended as a pain reliever. It says that Hanuman's image should be kept in oil till the pain disappears.[13]

VI HANUMAN AS *BRAHMACARI*

Hanuman is considered a celibate folk god. This characteristic is related to his devotion to Rama. So well established is Hanuman's celibacy that he has become a symbol of *brahmacarya* (sexual abstinence). There is popular folk belief in some regions of India that women should not come close to Hanuman's effigies.

The celibate Hanuman however, is a strikingly masculine and virile god, a symbol of masculine power. He is immensely strong in iconographical representations and is usually portrayed with a simian face. He is a Hercules with bulging muscles and a gigantic club. He is considered the patron deity of wrestlers and his prowess as a warrior is glorified in the *Ramayana*. By the beginning of the seventeenth century A.D., Hanuman emerged as a brahmacari god. He remains a virile and energetic male god bereft of female companionship. He is called *kumara brahmacari* by the *Ananda Ramayana*.[1] Ramadasa, the 17th century *brahmacari* saint of Maharashtra ,praises him as a widely known *brahmacari god*.[2] The Marathi *Bhavartha Ramayana* states that Hanuman was born with *koupina* (protective sheath for the male organ) on his person.[3] In the 'Hindu' *Padam Purana*, he revives Satrughana with the power of his *brahmacarya*.[4] His status as a *brahmacari* folk god of power in North India and Maharashtra, merits consideration. His celibacy is not accepted in all Indian and non-Indian traditions, the Jains deny him a celibate image.

His *brahmacarya*, although not specifically stated in *Ramayana*, is implicit in his character development in the epic. He is the trusted servant of Rama who entrusts him with the delicate mission of finding his wife. When Hanuman enters the *antapura* (inner women's quarters) of Ravana in search of Sita, he becomes disturbed on seeing other women sleeping in a dishevelled state. He fears that this might cause a moral lapse *(dharm lopa)* in his character[5] but is relieved when he finds that his glances towards the women do not arouse his sexual passions. He is thus capable of exercising self-restraint,[6] a true test of *brahmacarya*. Lawrence Babb correctly points towards the ancient correlation between sexual restraint and acquisition of power in Indian tradition.[7] O'Flaherty observes that " In texts the point is again and again made that great force is concentrated when the seed is drawn up."[8] Babb gives the example of Hanuman to establish the link between chastity and power, "Hanuman is absolutely chaste in his devotion to Rama, and as a result of this he has become a deity who presides over chastity."[9]

Hanuman's links with Rama as an incarnation of Visnu not withstanding, he becomes a *rudravatara* in the Saivite tradition. Here too his status as a *brahmacarya* god remains intact. The *Skanda Purana* mentions that the Sivalinga has become active and is capable of bestowing *Kamaprada* (wishes) due to the *brahmacarya* of Hanuman.[10] Hanuman's *brahmacarya*, however, is denied by Jaina writers. In the *Paumacariyam* and *Padam Purana*, Hanuman has hundreds of wives.[11] He marries Satyawati, the daughter of Varuna and Anangkusuma, Nal-Nandini, Hari-Malini, the daughters of Chandranakha and Padyaraga Sugriva.[12] Hanuman enters Lanka and gets enamoured of Lanka Sundari, the daughter of Vajramukha. He then has sex with her.[13]

The Valmiki *Ramayana* once refers to a gift of sixteen maidens as his wives, *(subhacarya bharyah kanyastu sodasa)*, given to Hanuman by Bharata on hearing the news of Rama's victory over Ravana.[14] The text, however, is silent on whether Hanuman actually married them. The *Adhyamta Ramayana* also refers to the above gift.[15]

More significantly, the *Ananda Ramayana* mentions Hanuman's son who was born to him inadvertently. To extinguish his tail set on fire by Ravana, Hanuman dived into the sea. A fish in the sea consumed drops of his *sveda* (perspiration). The fish conceived and the son who was born was called Makaradhvaja.[16] A similar story about Hanuman's son is mentioned in the 20th-century drama *Prasanna Hanumana Nataka* wherein Hanuman, not knowing the existence of his son denies their father-son relationship. When confronted by his son in *patala* (the nether world), Hanuman insists that he is a celibate, therefore, cannot have a son. Eventually, after knowing the real story of his son's birth he acknowledges Makaradhvaja as his son.[17] The two stories, in fact, reinforce Hanuman's celibacy.

Hanuman's sexual *liasions*, however, are frequently mentioned in the South East Asian Rama stories. Hanuman's *liasion* with the queen of fishes is mentioned. Hanuman is depicted as having *ramana* (sexual affair) with Svayam Prabha (*Apsara vanari*) and Mandodari (wife of Ravana).[18] The *Seri Rama Katha* mentions Hanuman's sexual exploits with Kekai Devi the daughter of Vibhisana and second wife of Lava.[19]

One way to resolve the puzzle of Hanuman's celibacy is to delve into the Valmiki *Ramayana* for clues. It is likely that a local, possibly celibate, male monkey god was used by Valmiki to enrich his epic by making him subservient to Rama. In other words, a local monkey god was absorbed into the *Ramayana*. Since there is no specific mention of Hanuman's sexual life in the Ramayana, later writers freely developed the theme of Hanuman's celibacy. It is interesting to note that dramas are also silent on Hanuman's *brahmacarya*. However, by the medieval times and in his modern manifestations, Hanuman, the folk-god, is linked to celibacy which is considered to be a source of power.

PART TWO

I HANUMAN IN SANSKRIT DRAMAS

This part of the work deals with the development of the Hanuman theme in Sanskrit drama from the fourth century A.D. to the present day. The approach is thematic. A 20th-century Sanskritic drama about Hanuman is chosen since Hanuman is studied through modern folklore and practices. Using the description of Hanuman found in the *Ramayana* of Valmiki, the development of the Hanuman theme in subsequent literature is analysed. The various facets of Hanuman's character, his exploits against the enemies of Rama, his role as a learned person, his devotion to Rama and his role as an envoy of Rama and Sugriva are discussed.

Hanuman's Exploits

In keeping with the general description of Hanuman in the *Ramayana* of Valmiki, playwrights constantly refer to him as a great warrior, a man of prodigious strength and wondrous military feats. He is called *Vira,*[1] *Mahavira,*[2] *Tribhuvana Kavira,*[3] *Vikramprakama,*[4] *Mahabala,*[5] *Mahabaho,*[6] *Viragrani,*[7] and *Amaybalsali.*[8]

Childhood Exploits

Valmiki mentions that Hanuman's mother Anjana was assured by the wind god that he was bestowing a child upon her who would be famous in the three worlds and perform miraculous deeds.[9] With this god inherited strength, Hanuman performed childhood exploits which even the gods did not anticipate. After his birth, says Valmiki, Hanuman leapt towards the rising sun mistaking it for a red fruit. The terrified sun went to Indra. Hanuman chased him to Indra's abode.[10] Indra, annoyed by this behaviour, hurled a thunderbolt towards the baby Hanuman and wounded him in the jaw. The dramatists essentially develop, with some variations, this and other themes of Hanuman's exploits ascribed to him in the *Ramyana.* The *Prasanna Hanuman Nataka* mentions how Hanuman acquired his strength through his being the son of wind god, how he was blessed further by the sages[11] and how after his birth, he leapt towards the sun to catch it, (also mentioned in the *Saugandhi Ka Haran Nataka).*[12]

In the *Mahavira Caritam Nataka* Hanuman performs similar miraculous acts as a child.[13] The dramas thus assign Hanuman semi-divine attributes and describe him as a child prodigy.

Crossing the Ocean

In Valmiki's *Ramayana*, a dramatic event which shows Hanuman's valour and strength is his crossing the ocean in search of Sita. Hanuman is the only person deemed fit by Rama to perform this arduous task. He goes towards the South because it is surmised that Ravana has carried off Sita in that direction. In the *Anargha Raghava Nataka*, it is Laksmana who trusts Hanuman's courage and strength for this task.[14] In the *Prasanna Hanuman Nataka*, Rama feels that Hanuman is fit for the expedition to Lanka as he is incomparable in prowess.[15] Sugriva too is confident about Hanuman's ability to perform this task.[16]

According to the *Prasanna Hanuman Nataka*, seeing the vast ocean the whole army of monkeys sat dejected in the woods near the shore, not knowing what was to be done. Then Sampati, the vulture, told them of Lanka, its fortifications and its distance from the sea.[17] No monkey dares to come forward to cross the limitless and hazardous ocean. Finally Hanuman , crosses the ocean.[18] The *Anargha Raghava Nataka* mentions that Hanuman was the only brave one who could go to Lanka but he was liable to forget his valour due to the curse of Brahma.[19] According to the *Prasanna Hanuman Nataka*, Jambavant then prompts Hanuman by reminding him of his strength, skill and swiftness. Hanuman, now aware of his own unparalleled powers, prepares himself for the big leap.[20] However, according to *Hanuman Nataka*, Hanuman was not reminded about his valour by anybody. When he heard that Rama wanted someone to cross the sea, he volunteered to undertake the task. He boldly asserted that he could do it if he were permitted to do so.[21] Jambavant then discloses to Rama that Hanuman is really a *rudravatara* and everything is within his range of capability. Hanuman thus becomes the avatara of Siva in the Hanuman Nataka. The *Prasanna Hanuman Nataka* too makes him an avatara of Siva, a divine being possessing unlimited powers. Therein Hanuman gets ready for the expedition without giving a second thought to its consequences. Extremely confident of his prowess, he assumes a gigantic form and gets ready for the flight.[22]

The very first obstacle for Hanuman, according to Valmiki was the Mainaka mountain. He wants to push the mountain down with a stroke of his chest. Since the Mainaka mountain greets him as a friend and requests him to take a rest on its peak, Hanuman lightly brushes it with a finger and speed away.[23] The path was full of hindrances but Hanuman, in the *Hanuman Nataka*, sails smoothly without any impediment. Mainaka rises out of the ocean to welcome him. He accepts the greetings by touching the mountain with his feet and moves on.[24]

According to the *Prasanna Hanuman Nataka,* and *Maha Nataka*, Hanuman crosses the sea by menancing Surasa and killing Simhika.[25] According to Valmiki too, Hanuman's flight over the ocean is not without hurdles. On his way to Lanka, he is confronted by formidable *raksasas* (demons) like Surasa, Nagamata and Simhika, apparently appointed by Ravana to guard the outskirts of his capital. Valmiki further states that Surasa was sent as an obstacle by the gods to test Hanuman's strength and valour and to see whether he had sufficient skills to evade and overcome dangers.[26] Hanuman, of course, defeats all *raksasas* and approaches the coast of Lanka. In some dramas, Hanuman crosses over the ocean and reaches Lanka [27] without encountering any problem. According to the *Prasanna Hanuman Nataka*, Hanuman has to face another hurdle before entering Lanka. He has to encounter Lanka Puri, the guardian *raksasi* deity of Lanka. He hits the deity with his fists and nearly kills her. The guardian *raksasi* Lanka Puri then grants him permission to enter the city[28] and directs him towards the Asoka grove where Sita has been confined.[29]

Destruction of the Asoka Grove

Another heroic deed of Hanuman is the destruction of the Asoka grove. Hanuman is also shown as a master strategist. After tracing Sita, he feels that he should take some precautions which will aid him in achieving Rama's goal. Hanuman wants Ravana to negotiate with him but soon discovers that he can not approach Ravana in a friendly manner. How then is Ravana to be approached? The *Abhiseka Nataka* mentions that Hanuman thinks it is best to destroy the Asoka grove, the most beautiful and favourite spot in Ravana's palace, to attract his attention.[30] According to Valmiki, Hanuman wants to destroy the grove to engage the *raksasas* in battle, so that he can asses their fighting abilities. He can then plan battle strategies for Rama's future attack on Ravana. He soon draws the attention of the *raksasas* guarding Lanka by killing some of them.[31] In the *Abhiseka Nataka*, he uproots all the trees and destroys the entire Asoka grove leaving intact only that spot where Sita resides.[32] Ravana cannot believe the news of the destruction in Lanka, for he thinks that his citadel is well guarded by the powerful *raksasas*. Ravana then sends his army to capture Hanuman. Hanuman, fighting with trees and stones, defeats the brave *raksasas*.[33] In the *Prasanna Hanuman Nataka*, Hanuman lays the *raksasas* unconscious with his fist and tail.[34]

Killing of Aksa

Almost all dramatists and Valmiki mention Hanuman's killing of Ravana's son, Aksa, who is known to be a great warrior.[35] In the *Prasanna Hanuman Nataka*, Ravana, shocked by the news of the death of his son Aksa, faints.[36] After regaining consciousness, in the *Hanuman Nataka*, he is ready to kill Hanuman.[37] The *Hanuman Nataka* further adds that Ravana and other *raksasas*, out of nervousness and anger, start tearing his picture with their teeth.[38] In the *Prasanna Hanuman Nataka*, the fearful guardians of Lanka alert the citizens of Lanka about the attack of Hanuman on Lanka.[39]

According to the *Prasanna Hanuman Nataka*, Ravana sends his son Indrajit, whose power and valour equalled the *devatas*, to fight Hanuman. During the fight, Indrajit finds him a match no less than himself and realises that all his weapons have no effect on him.[40] As a last resort, he attacks him with the *brahma astra*. Hanuman knowing that no weapon can wound him allows himself to be captured just to obey the orders of Brahma.[41] Hanuman thus bound in chains, is presented before Ravana. The *Abhiseka Nataka* states that when the period of *brahma astra's* potency was over, he shook himself free and sat before Ravana. Pretending to be a humble emissary of Rama, he spoke defiantly to Ravana and greeted him as an equal. But before he finished his speech he hurled words of defiance at Ravana.[42] According to Valmiki *Ramayana*, Ravana gets extremely annoyed and wants to kill Hanuman at that very moment but Vibhisana intervenes and tells him that as a *duta* (emissary), Hanuman should not be killed.[43]

Ravana seething with rage, satisfies himself by setting his tail on fire. In the *Ramayana* Hanuman is taken around the whole city after his tail is set alight. It serves Hanuman's purpose. He surveys the whole city in broad daylight, something he was unable to do so before.[44] A lot of attention has been drawn towards Hanuman's lighted tail by Valmiki and dramatists. His lighted tail becomes the symbol of bravery and physical strength. The dramas mention that with his tail he sets fire to the whole city except Vibhisana's palace and the Asoka grove where Sita is residing. He kills the leaders of the brave *raksasas* and reduces the city to ashes.[45] The

Prasanna Hanuman Nataka mentions that the destruction caused by him creates so much chaos in the city that people abuse and curse Ravana for his evil activities which have led to this calamity. The whole city resounds with the painful cries and wails of the women of Lanka.[46]

The *Janaki Parinaya Nataka* states that after the destruction of Lanka by Hanuman, Ravana is terror stricken. He orders his army to block all roads to Lanka so that other *vanaras* may not enter.[47] In the *Hanuman Nataka*, Ravana, in his meeting with Angada in his palace, makes special enquiries about Hanuman's present whereabouts.[48] He feels that he can easily defeat Rama and Laksmana but that Hanuman is a difficult proposition. He, therefore, resolves to eliminate him first.[49]

Hanuman on the Battlefield

Hanuman displays extraordinary skills as a warrior on the battlefield in his combat with Ravana, his brother and his sons. The *Hanuman Nataka* gives a detailed account of the battle between Kumbhakarna and Hanuman. Hanuman exerts himself successfully on the battlefield the day he meets Kumbhakarna. Kumbhakarna is equally courageous and destroys many *vanaras*. Hanuman is enraged when he notices the killing of *vanaras*. He comes forward and catches hold of Kumbhakarna's *gada* (mace) and kills him, throwing his head towards the Himalayas.[50] However, according to other dramas it is not Hanuman who kills Kumbhakarna but Rama.[51] In the Valmiki *Ramayana* too, Rama is the cause of Kumbhakarna's death.[52]

Hanuman's fight with Kumbhakarna's sons, Kumbha and Nikumbha, is mentioned in the Valmiki *Ramayana.* Sugriva kills Kumbha whereas Nikumbha has an encounter with Hanuman. The battle between the two is one between two equals. Hanuman is unable to use the bow and arrow but Nikumbha takes the *parigha* (mace), and whirls it in the air. It hits Hanuman, shaking the whole city. Hanuman strikes a blow on the chest of Nikumbha with his fist and strangles him.[53] The *Janaki Parinaya Nataka* mentions three powerful *raksasas*, Devantaka, Trisira and Nikumbha, who were killed by Hanuman.[54] In the Valmiki *Ramayana*, he kills Trisira with the latter's sword. He does not spare even the most trustwothy, wise and reliable ministers of Ravana Durdhara, Prahasta and Mahaparva.[55] The *Hanuman Nataka* states that Ravana loses his most valiant and heroic warrior in this war.[56] The *Saugandhi KaHarana Nataka* states that Hanuman's valour in the battle shows that he is unmatched. Only Ravana is mentioned as an exception.[57] In the *Saugandhi Ka Harana*

Nataka , Bhima, impressed with Hanuman's extraordinary bravery, says that Hanuman's deeds of valour and bravery on the battlefield can never be forgotten.[58] In the *Ullagha Raghava Nataka* , Ravana and Mandodari can not help praising the unparalleled valour of Hanuman though they are remorseful about their own defeat.[59]

The Fight between Hanuman and Ravana

The Valmiki *Ramayana* describes the battle between Hanuman and Ravana but it has been ignored by dramatists. Seeing the carnage wrought by Hanuman, Ravana takes the field himself. Ravana strikes first, hitting Hanuman with his palm on the chest. Ravana's blows are very powerful and Hanuman is thrown back. He quickly recovers and strikes Ravana with his palm Ravana is able to withstand the blow but feels its impact so much that he says, " Ah, you are a worthy enemy." Hanuman replies, " I do not care for your compliments. I am ashamed that after my blow you are still alive. I will deliver another one and you will go straight to the abode of Yama."[60] Agitated by Hanuman's rebuttal, Ravana strikes him with his full might a second time. Hanuman becomes unconscious. Having incapicitated Hanuman temporarily, Ravana returns to Nila and engages him to fight. When he awakens, Hanuman observes the code of a warrior and refrains from attacking Ravana while he is fighting with Nila.[61]

The *Ramayana* describe the battle further. After his engagement with Nila, Ravana hurls his spear with full force at Laksmana, precipitating Laksmana's fall. Ravana, wanting to ensure Laksmana's death, tries to lift him but cannot because Laksmana becomes heavy. Seeing this, Hanuman becomes so furious that he gives Ravana a terrible blow on his chest. Ravana falls to his knees and blood pours out of all his ten mouths.Ravana is in great trouble.[62]He loses the battle as he is again struck by an angry Rama.Thus next to Rama himself, Hanuman emerges as the hero in the grand battle against Ravana.The dramatists are silent about this great fight. Only the *Anargha Raghava Nataka* describes the fight with Ravana but Ravana is pitted against Sugriva.[63]

The *Hanuman Nataka* describes the confrontation between Ravana and Hanuman with major modifications. On the battlefield, Ravana, hearing the death of his son Indrajit becomes very angry. He catches the *brahma sakti* and hurls it at Laksmana. Hanuman comes in between and catches the *sakti*.[64] The *sakti* does no harm to Laksamana as long as Hanuman remains on the battlefield. Hanuman is removed from the

The figure of Hanuman inscribed all over with the word Rama, Rajasthan.

Hanuman in folk style, Mss. Painting, 18th century, Chamba (H.P.).

Bharat transporting Hanuman to battlefield with his magic arrow, 19th century, Oudh school.

Hanuman holding a book and a Veena, 16th century, South India.

Hanuman tearing open his chest to show his devotion to Rama,
Lucknow, 20th century.

Hanuman doing obeisance to Rama and Laksmana, early 20th century, Amritsar, Punjab.

Five-headed Hanuman, 18th century, Jammu (Pahari school).

Hanuman in a rhythmic pose wearing a long dhoti in Maharashtrian style, 18th century, Maharashtra.

battlefield by Narada Muni and the *sakti* is released. Only Hanuman and Vibhisana, of all men in Rama's camp, remain alert and strong. Vibhisana takes a torch in his hand and walks around the battlefield along with Hanuman to comfort and assist the wounded. They find Jambavant wounded and in pain. Jambavant recognises Vibhisana's voice and asks him in a pitiful tone if he has seen Hanuman anywhere.[65] Without giving an answer to his question, Vibhisana wants to know why he has asked only about Hanuman on this terrible day. Why had he not shown the same concern for Sugriva, Rama and Angada? Jambavant replies that if Hanuman is alive than the whole army would come back to life, without him it is worthless.[66] Hearing such extraordinary praise, Hanuman appears before Jambavant who then starts breathing normally again. The author of the *Hanuman Nataka* of obviously wants Hanuman to rise above all other characters and occupy the centre stage at this traumatic moment in the play.

The author of the *Hanuman Nataka,* to further enhance the importance of Hanuman in this key battle, thickens the plot. Rama doubts the sincerity of Hanuman and feels that Hanuman should not have left his brother unattended when the latter collapsed wounded. Hanuman, hearing such remarks, immediately presents himself before Rama. He assures Rama that no task is impossible for him but he only wants Rama's permission for doing it.[67] This candid pledge makes Rama contemplate the next assignment for him. Rama confident of Hanuman's valour, strength and strong resolve is also aware that his zeal can generate chaos the moment he is given permission to accomplish a task.[68] After considerable deliberation, Rama allows him to bring only Susena, the physician, to cure Laksmana.[69] Susena is immediately brought by Hanuman along with the cot on which he is sleeping.[70] Hanuman is depicted as a hero with a sense of honour. He feels that it is his moral duty to return Susena safely back to his palace although he belonged to the enemy camp.

Hanuman's Satayojana Leap

Hanuman's *Satayojana* (hundred yojan) leap towards the Drona mountain to bring herbs has been recorded by all dramatists.[71] The *Prasanna Hanumana Nataka* gives a thrilling description of Hanuman's flight. Kalayavana, a *raksasa* servant, is sent by Ravana to intercept and slay Hanuman. He disguises himself as a sage and sits on the route of Hanuman. Hanuman asks him about the water tank. He directs Hanuman to a nearby tank, telling him that its water was good and potable.[72]When Hanuman enters the tank, a crocodile seizes his foot. Hanuman kills it but from its body a lovely Apsara arises.[73]She had been cursed to live in that form until her release was accomplished by Hanuman. This Apsara in gratitude for his kindness, warned Hanuman of the impending danger from Kalayavana.[74]Hanuman returned to Kalayavana and killed him.[75]

According to the *Hanuman Nataka*, Hanuman kills a *raksasi* disguised as a crocodile, Kalanemi disguised as a sage and a huge force of *raksasas* and *gandharvas* sent by Indra.[76]Hanuman, sent to collect the herbs on the Drona mountain, could not identify the herbs required by Susena as all were " shining like fire". Hanuman, wasting no time, Hanuman lifts the mountain places it on the tip of his tail and takes the leap back to Rama.[77] The *Prasanna Hanuman Nataka* states that Hanuman has to bring the herbs quickly because the properties of these herbs are effective only before sunrise.[78]In the Valmiki *Ramayana*, Hanuman goes to the Drona twice to bring the herbs but he does not encounter any obstacles on his journey. In the *Ramayana* episode, all the plants become invisible when he starts searching for them[79] and that is the reason why Hanuman brings the whole mountain.

Another problem encountered by Hanuman on his way back to the battlefield while flying over Ayodhya, is described by some dramatists. The *Prasanna Hanuman Nataka* states that Hanuman's rapidity of movement causes great commotion in the sky which makes Bharata suspect some foul play on the part of the *raksasas*. Bharata, therefore, discharges an arrow towards him which precipitates his fall. When Hanuman identifies himself, Bharata, realising the importance of Hanuman's mission immediately apologises and offers to launch him on an arrow so that he can reach Lanka instantaneously. Hanuman politely declines the offer and continues the flight on his own strength.[80] The author of *Hanuman Nataka* gives another version of the same episode. He mentions that Hanuman, attacked by Bharata, gets annoyed at this interruption. When Bharata apologises for his mistake, Hanuman wants to test the integrity and valour of Bharata. He requests Bharata to help him reach Lanka, pretending that he is completely exhausted.[81] Bharata gets ready to help him by launching him on his arrow. Hanuman declines this mode of conveyance as he is satisfied with Bharata's good attitude towards Rama. Thus overcoming all obstacles, Hanuman reaches Lanka in a fraction of a moment.[82] The element of miracle is introduced by dramatists to heighten the sense of wonderment but the traditional characteristics of Hanuman his devotion to Rama and ability to fly are retained.

There is another example of Hanuman's stupendous strength in the *Saugandhi Ka Harana Nataka* Hanuman sleeps on the path which Bhima has to cross. Bhima, confident of his physical strength, laughingly asks him to clear the way for him. If he does not, he says, he will step across it in the manner Hanuman jumped across the ocean (not knowing that it was Hanuman to whom he was addressing his comments).[83]

The *Mahabharata* mentions a variation of the same episode about Hanuman's valour and supernatural power.[84]

Bravery and undaunted courage are the hallmark of Hanuman in the drama literature. The *Mahavira Caritam Nataka* mentions that Hanuman's bravery is proverbial, as he had never shown his back on the battlefield whereas other *vanaras* had behaved otherwise.[85] The *Hanuman Nataka* says that Rama, pleased with Hanuman's valour and unmatched courage, used his effigy as an emblem on his flag.[86] Arjuna, the hero of *Mahabharata,* also used Hanuman's emblem on his flag.[87] The story of Arjuna's *kapidhavaja* is also found in the *Ananda Ramayana.*[88] The *Mahavira Caritam Nataka* mentions that *devatas* cannot deny Hanuman's courage and fortitude.[89] The *Saugandhi Ka Harana Nataka* says that Hanuman is unmatched in courage and boldness in the three worlds.[90] In the *Hanuman Nataka*, Hanuman's enemy, the *raksasa* Lohitaksa, praises Hanuman's bravery and feels that Ravana is inferior to him.[91] According to the *Ananda Ramayana*, all the brave on this earth are incarnations of Hanuman .[92]

II HANUMAN AS POLITICIAN AND MILITARY COMMANDER

Hanuman's role as a political and military strategist in the *Ramayana* is enhanced in Sanskrit drama. In the Valmiki *Ramayana* Hanuman introduces himself to Rama as a *duta* (envoy) of Sugriva. Soon he plays an important role as the *duta* of Rama sent to Lanka to locate Sita. Hanuman as the *duta* of Sugriva, secures an alliance with Rama for him when he finds that friendship with Rama can be valuable for fulfillment of Sugriva's objectives. On gaining the kingdom of Vanara, Hanuman finds Rama bewailing the loss of his wife and wandering through the forest like a madman in search of her. He understands that Rama and Sugriva are fellow sufferers, having lost their throne and wife respectively. Empathising with their predicament, he embarks on a plan to forge a friendship between the two.[1] That Hanuman empathises with Rama for the loss of his wife is clear in the *Hanuman Nataka*. He makes an assertion that for Rama's sake, he is capable of killing Ravana single-handed but being a minister of Sugriva he can do it only with the permission of his master (Sugriva).[2] Hanuman is then still a loyal servant of Sugriva.

The concept of loyalty to the master is highlighted in Sanskrit drama and the *Ramayana*. In some of the plays, Hanuman escorts Rama to Sugriva's palace, where he arranges a pact of friendship between the two on the condition that Rama should first secure the throne of Kiskindha for Sugriva. Sugriva would then help him get back his wife.[3] Rama accepts this proposal of Hanuman. Hanuman knows Sugriva's fickle monkey nature and fearing that he may change his mind any moment, makes the two sign a treaty of friendship. Hanuman thus acts as a resourceful and loyal subject of his king.

In the *Anargha Raghava Nataka*, however, it is not Hanuman but Guha who acts as a mediator. Rama sends the proposal of friendship to Sugriva and Hanuman through Guha.[4] Rama promises Sugriva the kingdom but is still undecided about whose side he should take, Bali's or Sugriva's. He weighs the pros and cons of an alliance with each of the two brothers and finally decides to ally with Sugriva who is weak, submissive and a person in dire need of help.[5] Moreover, Rama expects Sugriva to place the *vanara* army at his disposal as a prize for killing Bali.

Hanuman is depicted as pragmatically sizing up the political situation to help both parties fulfill their missions. The *Hanuman Nataka* mentions that without Sugriva's help, Rama, as he himself admits, would not have been able to win Lanka.[6]

As a *duta*, Hanuman has to be articulate. In the *Prasanna Hanuman Nataka*, in his very first meeting with Hanuman, Rama is so impressed by his convincing speech on behalf of Sugriva that he trusts him immediately[7] and moves towards making Sugriva his friend.[8] In the *Anargha Raghav Nataka* , Rama finds in Hanuman a person who can fight effectively against his enemies. He later chooses him for the military mission of locating Sita in Lanka.[9] Sugriva too is in favour of sending him on that expedition as he knows that he is a brave and wise leader.

Hanuman's role as a *duta* involves spying for his master. Both *Adbhuta Darpana Nataka* and the *Anargha Raghava Nataka* emphasise his role as a spy.[10] As a *duta*, it is not possible for him to gather reliable information openly. Assuming the tiny form of a mosquito, he enters Lanka. *The Valmiki Ramayana* mentions that since Hanuman is in an alien land without any knowledge of its topography, he hides himself in the city until night falls. He finds Sita guarded by vigilant *raksasis.*[11] In the *Abhiseka Nataka,* he remains hidden and slyly listens to the conversation of the *raksasis.*[12] The *Hanuman Nataka* mentions that Hanuman waits until he has assured himself that the woman whom he has identified as Sita, is really so. He then shows her the ring given by Rama. In order to convince her of his identity, he narrates the events that took place since her disappearance from the *Pancavati.*[13] He assures her that Rama is fully prepared to take revenge against Ravana and release her from imprisonment. Hanuman thus fulfills skillfully the first job of contacting Sita without endangering himself.

Hanuman, the trusted envoy and spy of Rama has a critical role to play. Rama has sent Hanuman as his ambassador to give an ultimatum for freeing Sita.Before delivering the ultimatum, he addresses Ravana, "Your majesty! How are you? O King, listen. I am Hanuman, son of Anjana and the Wind god.Rama has sent me to you".[14] The *Prasanna Hanuman Nataka* presents Hanuman as a very bold *duta* who openly states that he is the one who has wrecked Lanka and also reveals the purpose of his coming to the city.[15] According to the Valmiki *Ramayana,* a *duta* is not expected to provoke the recipient of the message while delivering it. A *duta* should employ a conciliatory tone.[16] However, in Sanskrit drama, Hanuman behaves arrogantly towards Ravana. The ultimatum is so fearlessly addressed and in blunt language that it enrages Ravana and he immediately orders Hanuman's execution. Hanuman, standing alone in the court fully aware of Ravana's powers to punish him, remains undaunted. According to the *Hanuman Nataka,* he does not show the courtesies required of an ambassador. Instead of giving Rama's message, he boasts about his strength and threatens to kill Ravana.[17] This attitude of the dramatist is due to the fact that in the *Hanuman Nataka,* he is not depicted as a *duta* rather his status has been upgraded as an incarnation of Siva who is capable of accomplishing whatever he wishes. According to the *Abhiseka Nataka,* Hanuman is very courteous to Ravana in the beginning [18] but gets provoked when Ravana heaps abuse on Rama. He warns Ravana that he will meet his doom at the hands of Rama very soon. He tells him that his master is on the way to destroy Lanka.[19] According to some of the dramas, Rama sends him on the singular miission of finding the whereabouts of Sita and not to engage in conversation with Ravana. Rama wants to find out about Hanuman's true powers.[20]

Valmiki's Hanuman is endowed with a perceptive mind, making notes of places and events which would be useful in the coming battle of Lanka. The search for Sita takes him to every nook and corner of the city and he studies it minutely. He takes note of the fortifications of the city, its wealth, military weapons and techniques of war. He gives a vivid account of all that he has seen.[21] According to Valmiki, Hanuman was a master of military strategy. He contemplates that if the diplomatic expedients *sama* (friendship), *dama* (bribe) and *bheda* (division) were to prove useless with the *raksasas*, he would resort to *danda* (force). Another example of his strategy is his reckoning that if the leaders of the *raksasas* were to be killed, the rest of the army would become weak. He studies the technique of war of the *raksasas* and assesses their military strength by ravaging the whole Asoka grove. True to his plans, he first kills many *raksasas* and then, picking on the leaders of the army, demoralises it.[22]

In the *Abhiseka Nataka*, he spreads panic among the people of Lanka by creating havoc. He does not spare Aksa, the son of Ravana. He thus paves the way for Rama's subsequent attack.[23] The *Abhiseka Nataka* rationalises Hanuman's destruction of Ravana's favourite Asoka garden. Hanuman destroys it because of frustration at his inability to convince Ravana to release Sita by fair and friendly means.[24] The brave *raksasas* assault him with their weapons but Hanuman is not frightened. Ravana's son Indrajit, in the end, comes to destroy him with the *brahma astra*. Hanuman cleverly outwits the enemy by feigning defeat and behaving as if he were struck by *brahma astra*. He deliberately allows himself to be captured, giving him an oppurtunity to ruffle Ravana with his boast.[25]

Indrajit presents the captured Hanuman in the court of Ravana, who is at a loss to understnad how a *vanara* could enter the city well guarded by *raksasas* equipped with heavy and powerful weapons. In the *Abhiseka Nataka*, Ravana exclaims, "Why, the city is not even accessible to gods".[26] In order to punish him, he orders his tail to be set on fire. Hanuman stands undaunted. According to Valmiki, he is tied with ropes and taken around the whole city with his burning tail. He bears every insult inflicted by the *raksasas* as he is paraded through the streets and lanes of Lanka.[27] Hanuman makes no attempt to escape from his captors. He deliberately remains silent, for he is an expert in military strategy. He knows that while moving through the streets of Lanka he will be able to see places which are otherwise inaccessible. Accomplishing his objective, he then teaches a lesson to the *raksasas*. According to the Valmiki *Ramayana*, he assumes a tiny form and frees himself from the ropes. Then he transforms himself into a giant and kills all the *raksasas* who attack him with iron bars. Leaping from one place to another, Hanuman sets Lanka on fire.[28]

Valmiki adds that Hanuman, after having collected invaluable information regarding the strength of the enemy in Lanka, comes to the conclusion that Lanka can never be won by a frontal assault of an army. Although Hanuman is apprehensive of Rama's success against the formidable *raksasas*, he cheers Rama because he is loyal to him. He tells Rama that victory over Lanka is an easily attainable objective and that he has nothing to worry about.[29]

The dramatists also reiterate Hanuman's ability as a great warrior and military strategist. According to the *Mahanataka*, Hanuman reports to Rama after his Lanka mission that Ravana became so scared of the impending invasion by Rama that he thought of running away to a safer place.[30]

In Sanskrit drama, Hanuman, as a true and loyal adviser to his king, admonishes and goades him towards the correct path. After attaining his kingdom Sugriva forgets the urgency of Rama's task. Hanuman knows well that this is due to the Sugriva's preoccupation with pleasures and his laziness. He draws Sugriva's attention to his promise and his ingratitude towards Rama. He also chastises him and reminds him of the fate of Bali, who was eliminated by Rama.[31]

Hanuman's political acumen is amply demonstrated by Valmiki. Vibhisana, disgusted with the unruly behaviour of Ravana, leaves Lanka and comes to Rama for refuge. Sugriva, Angada and the other monkey ministers doubt the motives of Vibhisana's alliance with Rama. Nobody is in favour of granting him refuge. Jambavant and Sugriva want to test the integrity of Vibhisana before allowing him to enter the camp. Hanuman rejects all the doubts about Vibhisana. He advises Rama that Vibhisana knows Ravana's war efforts and his unruly conduct. Vibhisana knows of Bali's destruction and Sugriva's installation on the throne. He has, therefore, "come here, anxious to gain favours from you."[32] Hanuman knows that the services of Vibhisana would prove to be of immense help in defeating Ravana. Information about the secrets of Ravana's fortifications and the strength of his army could be provided by none other than a deserter like Vibhisana. In the *Abhiseka Nataka*, Hanuman does not welcome Vibhisana with open arms. Hanuman accepts Vibhisana only beacuse Ravana had expelled Vibhisana for supporting Rama's reasons for attacking Ravana. When Sugriva objects to

Vibhisana's joining Rama, Hanuman convinces Rama that he was witness to Vibhisana rebuking and quarreling with Ravana for Rama's cause.[33] Hanuman hints at the valuable services which Vibhisana could render to Rama. Rama accepts Hanuman's proposal and welcomes Vibhisana to his camp by granting him amnesty. In the *Prasanna Hanuman Nataka*, Rama does not consult either Hanuman or any other adviser regarding Vibhisana's entry to his camp. Rama accepts him with the intention of finding out the secrets of Lanka.[34] However, most play-wrights, following the *Ramayana* version, state that it is only because of Hanuman's efforts that Rama accepts Vibhisana in his camp.

After the coronation of Sugriva, Hanuman remains with Sugriva as his minister. He always helps Rama at his behest. In the *Anargha Raghava Nataka*, Hanuman is not only a minister but also a military commander of the Kiskindha forces.[35] In the *Abhiseka Nataka* Hanuman takes the lead while marching to Lanka.[36] In the *Prasanna Hanuman Nataka*, however, Nila is the commander of *Kiskindha* army.[37] In the *Hanuman Nataka*, Hanuman is not described as a commander but is the one who unravels the secret of Indrajit's *yajna* and destroys it when it is about to be concluded.[38]

About Hanuman's formal knowledge of *arthasastra*, no clear mention is made in Sanskrit drama but examples of his political skill portray him as a person knowledgeable of statecraft.[39] In the *Ramayana*, Sugriva finds in him an intelligent person well acquainted with the niceties of time and place and having knowledge of the science of polity.[40] The destruction of the Asoka grove, the burning of Lanka and the acceptance of Vibhisana in Rama's camp are examples of his political and military skills. He has been called a *tatvajnana-kala-dharma-visesavata*.[41]

III HANUMAN'S INTELLECTUAL ACHIEVEMENTS

The duties of a wise counsellor and a military strategist entail a thorough grounding in *arthasastra* and *niti* texts. Hanuman's proficiency bespeaks his knowledge of these texts.

The local simple folk god Hanuman was Sanskritized by Valmiki to make him more acceptable to his cultured readers. A similar process of acculturation of the *yakkhas* (local folk gods) is witnessed in Pali Buddhist literature. The *yakkhas*, whom Buddha and his monks encountered, engaged in philosophical conversation with Buddha and other monks. Some *yakkhas* were malevolent spirits who challenged Buddha and his teachings while others were willing to be converted. An entire *sutta*, the *Yakkha Pannha Sutta* deals with the philosophical religious dialogues of the *yakkhas* with Buddha.[1] In the *Suttanipata*, the *yakkhas* Suciloma and Alvaka are eager to understand the problems of existance.[2] In the *Mahabharata*, there is a dialogue between Dharma yaksa and Yuddhisthara encompassing metaphysical, spiritual and cosmological enquiries.[3]

Hanuman has the attributes of an intellectual being with an analytical mind. In the *Ramayana*, he is called *Budimatam Varista, Vakyavid, Vakya-tatvajnana.*[4] He is bestowed with rare wisdom from childhood. The wind god promises his mother Anjana that she would bear a child of rare intellect.[5] He is gifted with intellect, perseverance and objectivity.[6] Later, the sun god grants him a boon that there would be none to compete with him in the knowledge of the sastras.[7] In Sanskrit drama, there is no mention of such a boon but Hanuman is a person with wisdom and insight. In the *Valmiki Ramayana*, Jambavant and Sugriva bear testimony to his knowledge and skill.[8] Jambavant calls him *sarva-sastra-vidam-vara.*[9] In the *Mahabharata*, he is a learned scholar for Bhima requests Hanuman to explain to him the four cycles of an age.[10]

Valmiki depicts Hanuman as a Sanskrit grammarian and a scholar. To learn grammar, Hanuman follows the sun god continually in all directions. In a very short period, he attains perfection in all the branches of grammar. Nobody can excel him in any field of knowledge.[11] In the *Saugandhi Ka Harana Nataka* too, Hanuman emerges as a grammarian and a learned scholar, learning grammar from the sun god.[12]

Hanuman is an accomplished linguist too. According to the Valmiki *Ramayana*, he understands the script that was prevalent in Kosala and reads the autograph of Rama, written in that script on the ring. He knows two literary languages, the *manusi Sanskrita* (colloquial Sanskrit) used by ordinary people in their daily life and the *dvijata Sanskrita* (refined Sanskrit) used by the elite. Hanuman, in his very first meeting with Sita, is nonplussed regarding the language which he should use for opening the conversation with her. He thinks, "If I were to speak pure Sanskrita like the Brahmanas, Sita may mistake me for Ravana and would become terrified. Therefore, I think that it is proper to use the language of the common man."[13] The drama's do not refer to his bilingual skills but his conversation with Sita is in Sanskrit.[14] In the *Hanuman Nataka*, he reads the scriptures in Sanskrit.[15]

Hanuman's oratory is illustrated in the *Ramayana*. His elegant, fluent and cogent speech influenced Rama greatly in the matter of admitting Vibhisana into the camp. He has no pretensions while making speeches and usually concludes with concrete suggestions for Rama.[16] In his encounter with Ravana in the palace, he appeals to Ravana's sense of dharma and tapas which has given him unequalled powers, also suggests to him that in his own interest he should neither molest another man's wife nor indulge in unrighteous acts unworthy of an intelligent person like him.[17] In the *Saugandhi Ka Harana Nataka*, Hanuman through his skillful arguments surprises Bhima who is highly impressed and convinced that Hanuman is a clever person and a good *vadi* (debator).[18]

Hanuman's first meeting with Rama and Laksmana is illustrative of his refined mannerisms. In the Valmiki *Ramayana*, he talks to them very politely and addresses them as *rajarsis* (kings among sages). He speaks with appropriate movements of his limbs. His polished and courteous behaviour impresses Rama so much that he becomes confident that a person like Hanuman will win over even his enemy.[19] In another instance, he inspires confidence in Sita about his sincerity, not merely by giving her Rama's signet ring but also by making flattering references to Rama's greatness and noble character. In the *Ascarya Cudamani Nataka* he gives a very detailed description of the special features of Rama, one which only a thoroughly articulate and intelligent person can give. Hanuman describes the mental state of Rama and his agonizing love for Sita in such detail that Sita actually visualizes a clear picture of her husband in that state.[20]

In the *Prasanna Hanuman Nataka*, Hanuman has the same refined manner of speech. He wins the confidence of Rama by his civil manners and elegant use of language.[21] The offering of salutations on every occasion is an indispensable part of Hanuman's behaviour and it indicates his familiarity with etiquette. When he meets Sita in the Asoka grove for the first time, in pleasing mannerisms he addresses her respectfully as *patimaha, rajsute, jayatvacidhva* [22] and salutes her with folded hands.[23] He is courteous to friends and foes alike.[24] When he enters the palace of Ravana to deliver the message of Rama, he first greets him and enquires about his welfare before delivering the message.[25]

The statements attributed to Hanuman in drama are replete with elegant phrases indicate that he was well-versed in the *alankara sastra*. He describes Sita's presence amongst the black and ugly *raksasis* as "a streak of lightning among thick clouds."[26] Sita's thin and weak face looks "like a bunch of lotuses burnt in the sky."[27] In the *Ramayana*, Sita is like a *smrtimiva samdigadam* (memory full of doubts), *rdi nipatitamiva* (fallen fortune), *vihatamiva srdham* (lost confidence or respect), *as a prtihatamiva* (hope frustrated), *sopasargama yatha sidhim* (successes marred by obstacles), *budhim sakulsamiva* (intelligence perverted), *amutenapavadena kirti nipatitamiva* (fame destroyed by false imputations), *amryana moyogen vidyamprsithilamiva* (learning weakened by want of practice), and *samkararena yatha hinam vacamarthamtaram gatam* (words carrying different senses on account of wrong grammar).[29]

In the *Hanuman Nataka*[30] and the *Prasanna Hanuman Nataka*, Hanuman has knowledge of medicinal herbs and plants but is not a physician. Rama deputes him to fetch medicinal herbs to revive Laksmana. When Hanuman reaches Dronacala, he finds all the herbs glowing alike. Not recognising the plants required by Susena, the physician, he brings the whole mountain to Susena.[31]

Hanuman also admires and understands music. Staying at the Gandhamardana *vana* (forest), Hanuman hears the Kinnaraganas sing in praise of Rama and is completely lost in the music.[32] According to the *Hanuman Bhima Samvada* in the *Mahabharata*, Hanuman enjoys *Ramayana gayana* (songs) every day.[33] Hanuman's love of music, especially Rama's songs, complements his devotion to Rama. Hanuman is called the *pramukha pravartaka* (chief innovator) of *sangita sastra* in the *Sangita-Parijat*. It is believed that he is one of its composer *acaryas* (teachers) along with Sardula and Kahala.[34] In the *mangala carana* of the *Anupa Sangit Ratnakara*, Hanuman is mentioned as one of the eight *parama* (foremost) *acaryas* of Sangita Sastra.[35] In the *Tantrasara*, Hanuman is called an *adhisthata* (master) of music. In this text, Siva mentions to Parvati that one attains perfection in music by worshipping Hanuman.[36] Saranga Deva (c. 1300 A.D.) in his text *Sangita Ratnakara* mentions Hanuman with other *sanigita acaryas*.[37] In medieval texts on music, Hanuman is described as expressing his views on *ragas* (melodies). Sarda Tanya (c.1300 A.D.) in the *Bhava Prakashan*, quotes Hanuman's views about *anuraga cinha* and *rupak vises.*[38] Tikakara Kallinatha (c. 1500 A.D.) discusses Hanuman's views on *desiragas* (local musical compositions)[39]. King Raghunatha (c. 1700 A.D.) of Tanjore, in his text *Sangita Sudha*, states that Hanuman composed the *Laksiya Virudha Sastra.*[40] Medieval treatises on music containing his views are named after him. There is a reference to a text called the *Anjaneya Samhita* or *Hanuman samhita* but it is now lost.[41] The dramas and the *Ramayana*, however, are silent on this aspect of Hanuman's accomplishments.

Hanuman's love of music has not been understood properly. Music generates emotion in the listener and the singer. Music transcends baser feelings when one is fully engrossed in it. Perhaps, Hanuman learnt music to successfully perform Rama *bhakti*.

Hanuman, like Vidyadhara, possesses a knowledge of magical charms. According to the *Saugandhi Ka Harana Nataka*, he guides Bhima to the magical lake when he comes to Gandhamardana forest in search of the mythical flower demanded by Draupadi. He explains the magical charms to Bhima.[42] Directions given by Hanuman aid Bhima in unravelling the *gupta maya* (secrets and mysteries of the yaksas and their magical lake. Such details are not found in the *Mahabharata* which states only that Hanuman directed Bhima to the Magic lake.[43] Valmiki and some playwrights are silent on Hanuman's knowledge of magical charms.

The *Saugandhi Ka Harana Nataka* refers to Hanuman's psychic powers. To secure magical charms for Bhima in the Gandhamardana forest, he enters a yogic trance. Through his *siddhi* (psychic powers) he produces the object of Bhima's desire.[44] He can assume any form at will. He can fly without wings. He can also uproot mountains and carry them on the tip of his tail. Hanuman is proficient in eight kinds of *siddhis*. In the *Skanda Purana*, he manifests himself in his divine form on the request of Brahmans.[45]

Hanuman has the capacity to philosophically mitigate others' sorrow. According to the *Hanuman Nataka*, he revives Rama by his words of consolation when Rama grieves on the battlefield for his wounded brother Laksmana.[46] In a philosophical mood he advises Sugriva that he should leave those worldly pleasures that bring pain and misery in life.[47] In the Valmiki *Ramayana* he comforts Tara when she is overwhelmed by grief on the death of her husband Bali. He says that she should not mourn his death as Bali had been righteous, generous and patient and was sure to go to the world of those who had practised dharma.[48] In the *Prasanna Hanuman Nataka*, Hanuman philosophises about death and advises Tara to face it with courage.[49]

Hanuman is depicted as a scholar and musician in an unusual South Indian bronze piece, holding a *vina* in his right hand and a book in his left. It is also believed that Hanuman grants the prayers of students and scholars.[50]

IV HANUMAN'S RAMA *BHAKTI*

In the *Ramayana*, Hanuman's loyalty to Rama is emphasised. Hanuman is the archetype of the loyal follower who has immense trust in love for his master. These qualities of Hanuman are later developed into the theme of Rama *bhakti*. In the Rama *bhakti* tradition, devotees concentrating on god Rama, obtain spiritual solace and freedom and ultimately, union with god. Rama *bhakti* appears in *Uttara Kanda* (a later text not attributable to Valmiki)[1] where Hanuman prays to Rama to grant him boon of Rama *bhakti*.[2] However, even in the *Uttara kanda*, the notion of loyalty is the predominant one. The dramas also do not attribute any boon of Rama *bhakti* to Hanuman. However, he is a faithful follower, *duta* and a devotee paying undivided attention to Rama. He becomes a true devotee of Rama the day he meets him. He dedicates his life to the service of Rama. To rescue Sita from the clutches of Ravana is difficult because she is kept at a place where no one can reach her without thorough information about that territory. Whereas other characters show their helplessness owing to one reason or another, Hanuman eagerly awaits orders from Rama to proceed towards Lanka. [3]In the *Prasanna Hanuman Nataka* and the *Hanuman Nataka* he consoles the grief stricken Rama and assures him of success in his endeavour to find Sita.[4] However, he can succeed only with the help of and by grace of Rama.[5] Hanuman leaves no task undone. This task is full of hurdles and challenges but Hanuman faces it cheerfully and bravely. In the *Ascarya Cudamani Nataka*, he looks all around and finds Sita nowhere. Unable to find her, he is dejected and lapses into unconsciousness. After he regains consciousness, he is full of hopes again and continues his search.[6] In the *Prasanna HanumanNataka*, his sense of duty and devotion is evident from his determination to give up his own life if he cannot find Sita, for his life is worthless without fulfilling his duties towards Rama? In the *Prasanna Hanuman Nataka*, to fulfill Rama's undertaking, Hanuman allows himself to be captured by Meghanatha, the *raksasa*. For him, he is ready to bear insults.[8] On the battlefield he intercedes and bears the *brahma sakti* to save Laksmana, Rama's brother. In the *Hanuman Nataka*, Hanuman comes to Rama's rescue when he is depressed and looking for Hanuman's help to save his unconscious brother. He manifests himself instantly and assures Rama that he need'nt worry any more, now that he was there.[9] He can perform any formidable task but he cannot bear his master wearing a gloomy look.[10] In the *Hanuman Nataka*, he urges Rama to trust the *vanaras* who are at his beck and call and states that he, in the fraction of a sceond, will bring herbs required for curing Laksmana.[11]

In the *Ullagha Raghava Nataka*, Hanuman is proud to be in the service of Rama. Knowing the capability and devotion of Hanuman, Jambavant suggests that Rama send Hanuman to the Drona mountain to bring the medicinal plants. Rama is not in favour of sending Hanuman because he feels that he should not be troubled further, as he had done enough work for him. Hanuman, on the contrary, takes pride in rendering this service to Rama.[12] In the *Hanuman Nataka*, he stands with folded hands before Rama and says with humility that an ordinary *vanara* like him can do nothing except jump from one tree to another, things get accomplished only by the grace of Rama.[13]

As Rama's follower, Hanuman is concerned about Sita's plight and is always mindful of her welfare. The manner in which he conveys the message of Rama to Sita reveals his devotion to him. In the *Ascarya Cudamani Nataka*, he convinces Sita that he is the messenger of Rama by realistiacally narrating the sorry of plight of Rama after their separation. Initially, Sita does not believe that he is a messenger of Rama. She thinks that his speech is another cunning trick of Ravana. The answers of Hanuman convince Sita about his sincerity.[14] Hanuman then tries to console and cheer her but she is riven with doubt and apprehension, thinking that something was wrong with Rama since he had not come to rescue her personally. Deftly, Hanuman communicates to Sita, Rama's love and longing for her.[15] Only a true devotee of Rama can convey such private sentiments to his wife.

In the *Abhiṡeka Nataka*, Hanuman contemplates the method of convincing Sita that he is a genuine messenger of Rama, without frightening her.[16] In the *Ascarya Cudamani Nataka*, he consoles the "grief choked" Sita by describing Rama's grief stricken condition.[17] In the *Hanuman Nataka* and *Anargha Raghava Nataka*, he tells her that Rama is coming to resuce her with an army of *vanaras*.[18] The Hanuman of *Abhiseka Nataka* cannot tolerate Ravana's attempted seduction of Sita by persuasion.[19] He cannot bear a single dishonourable word uttered against Rama by Ravana. He gets ready to kill Ravana when he hears him calling Rama a *gatayu* (deceased) and *srngala* (jackal). He cannot suppress his anger and insults Ravana openly in his court.[20]

According to the Valmiki *Ramayana*, Hanuman while assuring Sita of the impending arrival of Rama along with the *vanaras*, thinks that the best way to put an end to the pitiful plight of Sita is to carry her on his back to Rama. He persuades her to accept his proposal.[21] In the *Prasanna Hanuman Nataka*, Hanuman worships Sita [22] while in the *Ascarya Cudamani Nataka*, he sings songs of her glory.[23] In the *Ascarya Cudamani Nataka*, however, Hanuman becomes indifferent to her during her fire ordeal although he knows that she is pure and chaste woman. He is perplexed on seeing her pristine calm, something entirely different from what he had seen in Lanka. He pays no heed to her requests and pleas and even refuses to listen to her. With a perturbed mind, he consents to Rama's decreeing of the ordeal for Sita.[24] The Hanuman of the *Abhiseka Nataka* also behaves in the same manner.[25] In the above two instances, Hanuman is caught in a conflict of loyalties. He finds Sita's purity convincing but his primary sense of loyalty towards Rama is absolute. His devotion to Rama ultimately takes precedence over his devotion to Sita. He sees Sita not as a separate individual but as an extension of Rama.

In the *Ullagha Raghava Nataka*, Hanuman fully sympathises with Sita. He knows that she is pure but is helpless. He cannot question the wisdom of his master. Instead, he blames Sita's ill luck.[26]

Sita too has great affection for Hanuman because of his association with Rama. Valmiki mentions that she finds in him alone an amalgam of innumerable good qualities. He is valiant, skilled, humble and firm.[27] She wants to reward Hanuman for bringing the news of Rama's victory. She says, "If I had gold in abundance and precious stones, if I had all the kingdoms of the three worlds to give, they all would not make up an adequate reward for the message you have brought me."[28] *The Saugandhi Ka Harana Nataka* states that after the coronation ceremony of Rama all the guests departed with their gifts but Hanuman continued to stand there with folded hands. Sita, as an acknowledgement of his services, presented him a pearl necklace which had been given to her by Rama.[29]

Hanuman not only reveres Rama and Sita but also their devotees. In Lanka, when Hanuman learns of Vibhisana's devotion to Rama and finds that his house is marked with Rama's name, he avoids setting it on fire.[30]

In the dramas, Hanuman emerges as an exceptional devotee of Rama. He wants to serve his master all the time. In the *Dutangada Nataka*, finding his master tired, Hanuman massages his feet.[31] In the *Prasanna Hanuman Nataka*, always humble in his presence and devoted to him. Hanuman wants to be near always him.[32] In the *Anargha Raghava Nataka*, he feels restless in his absence.[33] In the *Mahavira Caritam Nataka*, he constantly bows his head before his master.[34] The *Prasanna*

Hanuman Nataka says that although Hanuman is eager serve his master Rama, he never expects to be rewarded for it.[35] The *Hanuman Nataka* mentions that once when Rama embraces him out of gratitude, he says that he does not deserve such high praise.[36] He feels that it is Rama's grace that prompts him to do a job.[37] In the *Prasanna Hanuman Nataka*, he worships Rama as an incarnation of Narayana.[38] He always invokes his name before commencing work.[39]

Such was Hanuman's *bhakti* that he is credited with the composition of the first Rama katha known as either *Maha Nataka* or *Hanuman Nataka*. The katha has come down to us in two versions [40] *Hanuman Nataka* and *Maha Nataka*. Both versions state that Hanuman is the original author. The concluding verse in Damodar Mishra's version states that the work was composed by the son of the wind god (Hanuman) who deemed it to be *amrtabuddhya* (ambrosia). It was later recovered by King Bhoja and edited by Damodar Mishra.[41] Mohandasa, the commentator of the drama, explains that Hanuman wrote this work and engraved it with his nails on the rocks. Valmiki recognised its excellence and was worried that it would eclipse his own *Ramayana*. The generous Hanuman to please Valmiki, threw it into the sea from which after a score of years, it was recovered by his avavara Bhoja with the aid of fishermen.[42]

A mere mention of Rama's name is enough to make Hanuman forget everything else in the world. In the *Kalyana Saugandhi Ka Nataka*, Hanuman and Bhima are locked in combat when a *vidyadhara* intervenes and conveys the message of Indra that they should stop fighting each other and live like the brothers Rama and Laksmana. The moment Hanuman hears the name of Rama he forgets the fight and starts narrating the characteristics of Rama to Bhima.[43]

The theme of Rama *bhakti* is sustained in Tulsidas's *Rama Carita Manas*. Kalanemi, the uncle of Ravana, is sent to the Drona mountain to prevent Hanuman from taking herbs for curing Laksmana. Kalanemi knows Hanuman's propensity for listening to Rama *katha* while doing work. Moreover, it is known that Hanuman never leaves a place until the completion of the recitation of the *Ramayana*. Kalanemi tries to stop Hanuman from carrying his assigned task by reciting the Rama *katha*.[44] Hanuman gets completely absorbed in it. He forgets everything else. Kalanemi, however, cannot continue his narration till the morning as he does not know the whole Rama *katha*. In order to keep Hanuman busy, he starts praising himself. Hanuman recovers the moment the *katha* comes to a halt. He immediately proceeds to the Drona mountain. In the

Tulsidasa *Ramayana*, Hanuman is the embodiment of Rama *bhakti*. Laksmana, Bharata and Hanuman are all devoted servants of Rama but Siva considers Hanuman to be the ideal devotee. Hanuman is revered because Rama lives in his heart. Bharata says, "Monkey, at the sight of you all my sorrows have passed away, for today, I have met in you my beloved Rama."[45] In the *Ananda Ramayana*, Hanuman requests Rama that he should always be present wherever the *Rama Carita* is being sung. There is a popular folk belief that Hanuman is always present wherever the Rama *katha* is sung.[46]

Another popular belief is that the name of Rama is engraved not only in the heart but on every part of Hanuman's body. For him, everything should be marked with Rama's name. His loyalty to Rama is held up as the example of faithfulness and self-surrender. In the *Saugandhi Ka Harana Nataka*, Bhima thus pays tributes to Hanuman, "When the great sages and munis failed to describe the greatness and nobility of Hanuman in words then how can an ordinary mortal like me sing his praise? I bow my head before that noble person who did wonderful deeds in the world."[47]

Hanuman subordinates his might to that of his lord, Rama, whose most ardent devotee he is. He exemplifies the essential quality of devotion complete surrender of oneself to the master. A remarkable passage is found in the *Hanuman Nataka* where Rama expresses his gratitude for the numerous services rendered by Hanuman. Rama says that he feels so much indebted that his own life is not enough compensation for all that Hanuman had done for him. Rama wants Hanuman's good deeds to be permanently etched in his heart.[48] The *Maha Nataka* mentions that Hanuman does not feel worthy of such a big reward for his ordinary service.[49] The *Abhiseka Nataka* says that for Hanuman, the true *bhakta* (devotee), Rama is the bravest, the master and lord of the world.[50] In the *Hanuman Nataka*, his master is unmatched and Hanuman sings poems of his glory.[51]

In the *Puranas* and modern sectarian religious tracts Rama *bhakti* is closely associated with Hanuman. Hanuman's Rama *bhakti* is stated in the *Bhavisya Purana* wherein Brahma confers the boon of Rama *bhakti* upon Hanuman.[52] According to the *Kurma Purana*, Hanuman's primary characteristic is his being a servant *bhakta* of Rama.[53] The *Siva Maha Purana* mentions that Hanuman is the founder of Rama *bhakti*.[54] Hanuman's Rama *bhakti* in the *Purana* is an expression of the same loyalty and devotion to Rama as depicted in the Valmiki *Ramayana*.

The *Ananda Ramayana* (medieval Ramayana) mentions the boon of

Rama *bhakti* to Hanuman[55] as in the Valmiki *Ramayana.* In the *Adhyatama Ramayana*, during the coronation ceremony of Rama, Hanuman asks for the boon that he would always chant the Rama *nama* (name of Rama).[56]

The transformation of Rama *bhakti* from devotion and loyalty to Rama to the pure devotion of a *bhakta* towards his god is a logical development. By the time of Tulsidas, Hanuman's Rama *bhakti* becomes a symbol of *bhakti* with the connotation of being a devotion to god.

Hanuman, more than any other character in the *Ramayana*, is the natural choice for the *bhakti* model because of his love for his master. In the later Rama *kathas,* therefore, Hanuman is not only a Rama *bhakta* but also an *acarya* (teacher) of Rama *bhakti*. In the *Rama Rehasiya Upanisada* (a late medieval work), Hanuman teaches the method of *Ramopasana.*[57] In modern times, *Rasika Sampradaya* considers Hanuman the *acarya* of *maduriya bhakti.*[58] In the *Hanumat Samhita*, Hanuman, in the disguise of Rama's friend Carusila, teaches Rama *bhakti* to Agastya.[59] This is a total fabrication but Hanuman is shown as the teacher of Rama *bhakti*. According to a folk belief, Hanuman is considered the *vyakta* (narrator), of regional *Ramayana* versions such as the *Saurya Ramayana* and *CandraRamayana.*[60] In the *Ramananda Sampradaya*, Hanuman is one of the principal *acaryas* of Rama *bhakti*. According to this work, it is believed that the *Sri Rama Tarak mantra* was given to Sita by Rama. Sita passed it on to Hanuman who gave it to Brahma[61] who spread the *mantra* further. Thus, modern traditions make Hanuman not only the model Rama *bhakta* but also the expounder of Rama *bhakti* through whom it becomes accessible to a devotee.

PART THREE

I HANUMAN IN TULSIDAS' *RAMA CARITA MANAS*

Hanuman's key role in Tulsidas' *Ramayana* is to serve Rama as his *dasa-bhakta* (servant devotee). Hanuman, according to Tulsidas, is Rama's true *bhakta*. His roles as Rama's trusted friend, ally, envoy and warrior, are of secondary importance to Tulsidas. Selected passages bearing on Hanuman's devotion to Rama have been translated herein-after. However there is the danger of treating the passages in isolation. Since the full context in which Hanuman appears in the various *kandas* of *Ramayana* cannot be given here. A short introduction is, therefore, provided for every encounter that Hanuman has with other key characters in the *Ramayana*. It must be reiterated that this translation is meant to highlight Hanuman's Rama *bhakti*.

This is not a critical English translation of the *Rama Carita Manas*, using extensive footnotes. The translation is in prose. Long sentences are broken into smaller ones. The translation cannot convey the resonance and lucidity of Tulsidas' original verses. However, Tulsidas is a peoples' poets who uses simple word structure in his poems. His poetry is so emotive that even a drab translation is able to convey his message of *bhakti*.

The English translation is based on the Hindi version of Tulsidas' *Rama Carita Manas* published by the Ramayana Press. The page numbers in the parentheses refer to the Ramayana Press edition.

Rama and Hanuman

It is in the *Kiskindha Kanda* that Hanuman first encounters Rama, who wandering in the forest in search of Sita. Sugriva, the King of apes, apprehends danger on seeing Rama and his brother Laksmana. He suspects that they are the deputies of brother Bali who have been sent to kill him. At the behest of Sugriva, Hanuman goes to meet Rama to investigate the real purpose of their presence in the forest. Hanuman assumes the *batu rupa* (guise of a young brahman student) when he encounters Rama.

Bowing his head in salutation Hanuman speaks thus, " Great warriors, both fair and dark in complexion, in Ksatriya regalia, I find you in the forest. You walk with your tender feet on this jagged soil. Why, tell me, are you wandering in this forest. You are delicate, handsome and of pleasing disposition and yet you are confronting the fierce wind and heat of this forest. Are you of the triad of gods Brahma, Visnu and Siva ? Or else are you one of the two *Nara-Narayana* ? Are you the Lord Creator, the Lord of all beings ? Are you his reincarnation as humans who have come to ward off the unhappiness and burdens of this world ?" (p. 575).

Rama replies " We are the sons of King Dasratha of Kosala. Obeying our father's wishes, we have exiled ourselves in the forest. We are two brothers Rama and Laksmana. Accompanying us was my beautiful bride Sita. She has been abducted by the *raksasas* . Brahman!, we are wandering in her search. We have introduced ourselves. Tell us about yourself" (p. 576).

Having recoganized the Lord, Hanuman, in abject surrender, falls on the feet of Rama. Siva, narrating this event to Uma, his wife, says, "Uma, Hanuman's happiness became unbounded, defying description. His body became infused with joy and trembled . He turned speechless. He kept on staring at them in admiration". Hanuman, recovering from his ecstacy praises Rama with heartfelt contentment, " Lord, it was correct on my part that I should enquire about you but why should you ask questions like a mortal. I wandered about, lost in myself, due to your magic. That must be the reason why I could not recognise the Lord. Dumb witted as I am, I am also a fool, callous at heart and ignorant. Then again, Lord, you, the saviour of the downtrodden, led me astray. Lord, I am full of shortcomings but the Lord should never forget his servant. Lord, the beings are spellbound by you, you control them. And only you can help them achieve their liberation. I solemnly affirm by my Lord's name that I know no other means of adoration except chanting your name. The servant lives securely if he has trust in his master; a child if he trusts his parents. The Lord supports his own devotees who trust him" (pp. 576-577).

Having said this, Hanuman assumes his real form and falls at Rama's feet. Rama raises Hanuman to his feet and embraces him . Tears of joy flowing from his eyes, he soothes Hanuman's feelings, "Do not loose heart, Hanuman. You are dearer to me than Laksmana. It is said by all, that I am of impartial bent of mind but a devotee is dearer to me because he looks not elsewhere for the path to his release ". Hanuman, the Lord reflects trusts me entirely. He is constantly aware that he is the servant and

I am the Lord, the master and that all the forms are Lord's creations." (p.577).

Hanuman senses that his master is favourably inclined towards him. Overcome with joy, he overcomes his discomfiture. He then tells to Rama, "Lord, on this mountain lives Sugriva, the King of apes. He is yours as a slave. Offer your friendship to him. Make him feel secure, for he is now under great duress. He will initiate the search for Sita by sending ten million apes in all directions." (p. 577).

In the *Kiskindha Kanda*, Sugriva despatches his ape army, ordering them to search Sita. Before starting on their mission, the apes bid farewell to Rama.

They bow their heads before Rama's feet and take his permission to leave on their mission. Full of joy they leave that place, with Lord in their minds. The last one to bow down his head in salutation is Hanuman. The Lord knows what Hanuman is about to accomplish for him. He summons him to come near him. He places his lotus like hand on his head, blessing him. He takes out his ring from his finger and gives it to him, his most trusted devotee. He tells him: " Do all you can to comfort Sita. Tell her of my prowess and my longings for her in my separation. Return with all haste." Hanuman was so enthralled that he felt that he had achieved his life's fulfillment. He went ahead on his mission his thoughts fixed on his gracious Lord (p.593).

Hanuman and the Apes

Jambavant, the ape general who urges Hanuman to go to Lanka, praises him when he ready to do so. This episode is in the *Sundara Kanda*.

"I salute Hanuman. He is the abode of matchless strength. He has a body like the golden Meru mountain. He consumes the *raksasas* like fire. He is perfect in wisdom. He is endowed with excellent virtues. He is the chief among the apes. He is Rama's beloved *bhakta*".

A pleased Hanuman tells the apes, "Brothers, look forward to my return. Bear with the sorrows of my departure by living on the roots, berries and fruit. I shall, in the mean time, return after seeing Sita. I shall complete my task. It causes me great delight in accomplishing this". He salutes all the apes. With Rama in his heart, enthusiastically he goes his way. (p.606).

Hanuman and Vibhisana

Hanuman arrives in Lanka and begins his search of Sita *(Sundara Kanda)*. He is surprised to see a temple of Hari with a *tulsi* plant in the land of the *raksasas*. The temple happens to be in Vibhisana's palace. Vibhisana has just awaken from his slumber.

Vibhisana chants the name of Rama. Hanuman instantly realises that he is a good and virtuous person. He is pleased. Hanuman reflects, " I will introduce myself to him on my own volition because my cause would not be damaged by such a good person". Appearing in the guise of a brahman, he hails him. Vibhisana gets up and goes to meet him. He salutes him and enquires about his well-being. He asks Hanuman " Are you one of the devotees of Hari for I feel an instant bond of affection for you. Are you one of those, who love to worship the feet of Rama, who have come to bless me ?" Hanuman then narrated the doings of Rama. While listening to the story, both become joyous. They get engrossed in contemplating Rama's supreme virtues (p. 611).

Vibhisana tells Hanuman, " Listen to me Hanuman, I am surviving in this place like a helpless being. I am likened to a tongue trapped between the teeth. Forlorn as I am, do you think that the Lord will ever take pity on me? My body is that of a *raksasa* and as such I have no rightfull means for cultivating devotion to Rama but now meeting you, Hanuman, I feel assured that without God's grace one cannot encounter a holy person. It is only on account of the Lord's wish that you have made yourself known to me" (p. 611).

Hanuman replies, "Listen to me, it is the Lord's way to always love his devotees. Look at me. Do I look like a member of high a born family. As a childish ape, I am the lowest born. If some one were to utter our name in the morning, he would have to go without food the rest of the day. As despicable as I am, the Lord has shown pity on me."

Contemplating the Lord's attributes, Hanuman's eyes fill with tears. Hanuman experiences a deep sense of calm by extolling the manifold virtues of Rama (p. 612).

Hanuman and Sita

Sita in captivity is shown in the *Sundara Kanda* as languishing

in the Asoka garden in Lanka. Her mood is dark and gloomy. She is desperate and thinking of commiting suicide.

Observing Sita experiencing severe pangs of separation from her Lord, Hanuman feels that every moment of Sita's torments was like an aeon. Hanuman muses for a while and then drops the ring from the tree. It is like a spark falling off the infernal Asoka tree. Sita enthusiastically picks it up. She looks at the charming ring on which is carved Rama's name. She is taken aback, for she recognizes it. She is overjoyed yet alarmed and worried. She reflects, "Who can dare conquer the unconquerable Rama? But no magic could make such a ring." She is vexed by such thoughts. Hanuman then speaks to her soothingly. Listening to Hanuman extolling the virtues of Rama, Sita's sorrows disappeared. With rapt attention, Sita listens to Hanuman's description of Rama's doings from the begining (pp. 616-617).

Sita tells Hanuman "Brother, why do you not identify yourself to me? You, who have narrated this story which is like nectar to my ear." Hanuman draws closer to her. Sita turns and seeing him sits down wonderstruck at his appearance. Hanuman says" Mother, I am a messenger of Rama. I am speaking the truth. I swear by Rama that I was the one who brought this ring. Rama has sent it for you as a mark of rememberance". Sita then asks, "Tell me, how men can be comrades of the apes". Hanuman then tells her how this alliance was forged (p. 616).

On hearing Hanuman's loving speech, Sita gains confidence. She realises that Hanuman is the servant of Rama in thoughts, words and actions. She recognizes a true devotee of God in Hanuman. Her eyes became wet with tears. She is intensely moved and shaken by this experience. She says, " Hanuman, you have come at the right time when I was about to sink in the sea of separation. Now tell me the news of the well-being of Rama, that abode of happiness, and his younger brother. Kind and merciful is the Lord. But why is he so indifferent towards me ? It is his nature to bring happiness to his servant. But does he ever remember me? Will I ever be blessed to see the Lord in his charming and fair form?" Sita becomes speechless and eyes full of tears remarks, "Lord you have forsaken me entirely". Seeing Sita's desolate condition, Hanuman gently consoles her. " Mother, the Lord and his brother are well but he is in great pain because of separation from you. Do not despair, Rama loves you twice as much as ever. Mother, now listen to Rama's message and take courage''. Having said this, Hanuman is overpowered with emotion and tears fill his eyes. He then conveys Rama's message to Sita, " Sita, the whole of universe for me has turned upside down due to our separation. The new leaves on the trees are like fire. The night is like eternal death. The moon is like the sun. A patch of water lillies looks like a forest of blades. And the clouds seem to rain hot oil. Those who are my well wishers, now trouble me. The cool, gentle and fragrant winds hissing like serpents. The pangs of sorrow become less by unburdening it. But in whom should I confide? No one is capable of knowing what it means. The real meaning of my love for you and yours for me, is known only to me. My heart is ever with you. My love for you is deeply rooted. Understand that this is so.'' (pp. 617-618).

As Sita listens to the message of her Lord, she becomes absorbed in love and loses consciousness of herself. Hanuman then says, " Take hold of yourself and remember Rama, who gives happiness to his devotees. Putting your trust in the power of Rama, pay attention to what I say and remove your fears. The army of the *raksasas* is like moths and Rama's arrow are like fire that consumes them. Know this to be true that the *raksasas* are as good as dead. If Rama had known about your whereabouts, he would not have delayed rescuing you. When Rama's arrows rise like the sun, how will the darkness of the *raksasas* army survive? This very instant, I can take you away from here. I swear by Rama that he has not given me permission to do so. Be patient for a few days more. Rama will come here with his apes, kill the *raksasas* and carry you away. Narada and other sages will then sing paens to his victory throughout the three worlds'' (p.618).

Sita tells Hanuman, " The apes are like you but the *raksasas* are very strong warriors. I have great reservations about the victory of Rama.'' Hanuman then reveals his true form. It becomes evident to Sita that he would be formidable in the battle and that he is exceedingly strong. Hanuman again resumes his small stature. Hanuman reassured Sita further, " Listen, the apes are not endowed with great strength or intelligence but due to the grace of the Lord, even a tiny snake can consume an eagle'' (pp. 618-619).

Sita is satisfied with Hanuman's speech which is full of devotion to Rama, rigorous and forceful. She gives him her blessings. Since she recognises that Hanuman is very dear to Rama she says,'' May you grow in strength and virtue. Grow not old and die. Let Rama be ever gracious to you''. When Hanuman hears the blessing, ''May the Lord favour you'', he becomes engrossed in the love of Rama. Over and over again Hanuman bows his head before Sita's feet and speaks to her with folded hands ''Now, I have fulfilled my duties. Also it is well known that your blessing is efficacious. Mother, looking at the delicious fruit on the trees, I am beginning to feel very hungry.'' Sita advises him, '' Be on gaurd. The garden is protected by the powerful and dreadful *raksasas*''. Hanuman replies, '' I do not fear them. But if satisfied (with my mission), give me permission to leave''. Sita convinced of Hanuman's strength and intelligence, says, '' Go, keep your mind engrossed on the Lord's feet. Eat the delicious fruit'' (p. 619).

Bharata and Hanuman

In the *Lanka Kanda*, Laksmana is mortally wounded in the battle with Ravana's son, Meghanada. The only way in which he can be revived is throughout the application of herbs found on the mountain of Dronagiri. Rama asks Hanuman to fetch the herbs. Hanuman goes to the mountain but not being able to identify the herbs, uproots the mountain and holding it in his hand, flies back. He passes over the city of Ayodhya on his way.

Bharata sees a huge figure in the sky and guesses that it is a *raksasa*. He pulls the bowstring to his ear and shoots an arrow without its tip. The arrow strikes Hanuman and he falls unconcious on the ground chanting, ''Rama, Rama''. When Bharata hears this dear name being chanted, he dashes to the place with haste. Seeing Hanuman in torment, he holds him near his chest and does his utmost to revive him but of no avail. He becomes crest fallen. He reflects on this event, with eyes full of tears '' God, who made me hurt Rama, has once again put me in this distressful condition. If in thought, word and action, I have unsullied love for Rama's lotus like feet and if Rama is graciously inclined towards me, then let the ape be revived from his pain and tiredness.'' Hearing this solemn utterance Hanuman sits up and hails Bharata, ''Glory, Glory be to the Lord of Kosala''. Bharata joyously embraces Hanuman. Bharata is enthralled and his eyes fill with tears. As he remembers Rama, he can scarcely control his love for him. He says, ''Tell me friend, how Rama and his brother and Sita are faring? '' Hanuman told him all that had transpired. Bharata becomes sad. He says, ''God, why was I born into this world? I have not been of any use to the Lord''. Realising that this is not the time for lamentation, Bharata calms himself and tells Hanuman, " you will be late in reachimg Lanka and your efforts will come to a nought. Hence, mount on my arrow with your mounatin and I will make sure to send you where Rama is." Hearing his words, a conceited Hanuman wonders how will it be possible for Bharata's arrow to travel with his weight on it. But recollecting the power of Rama, he salutes Bharata's feet and with folded hands says, "Master, I shall affix your mighty power on to my heart and shall then be able to go swiftly to my destination." Again saluting Bharata, Hanuman takes his leave. As he sets forth, Hanuman repeatedly praises in his mind the power of Bharata, his virtues, qualities and endless devotion to the feet of Rama (pp. 705-706).

In the *Uttara Kanda*, Rama, having killed Ravana and rescued Sita, sets out on his journey back home. Rama travels in his Puspaka aeroplane. He instructs Hanuman to assume the form of a brahman student and enter the city of Ayodhya and ask him to inform Bharata that all is well with him, his brother and Sita. Hanuman immediately sets out on his journey to Ayodhya. The people of the city eagerly await Rama's return. Bharata is the most excited person.

As Bharata's mind is drowning in the sea of separation from Rama, Hanuman arrives (in brahman form) like a raft to save him. Hanuman observes Bharata sitting on a bed of *kusa* grass, with matted hair, looking frail and constantly chanting, "Rama, Rama,". Tears are streaming from his eyes. Hanuman, seeing him in this state trembles with great joy. Tears begin to flow from his eyes. His mind is enveloped in a serene happiness. Bharata's (chanting of Rama's name) was like ambrosia to his ear. Hanuman says, " He, whose separation you lament night and day and whose cumulative virtues you sing endlessly, the pride of the lineage of the Raghus, the bestower of happiness to the good, the saviour of the gods and sages, is coming back in safety. The Lord is coming to the city accompanied by his brother and Sita." Bharata when he hears this news, forgets all his sorrows, like a thirsty person does on finding water. He asks Hanuman, "Who are you? Where have you come from ? You have brought me welcome news". Hanuman says," I am an ape, the son of the wind god and my name is Hanuman. I am the servant of Rama who is an ally of the needy". Bharata rises from his seat and embraces him with honour. As he embraces him, his love for him knows no bounds. Tears roll from his eyes and body trembles with uncontrollable feelings. Bharata says, " Hanuman, your presence here has dissipated all my sufferings. It is as if I have met my beloved Rama.'' Repeatedly, Bharata asks how Rama has fared. He then tells Hanuman '' Hear me out, Hanuman. What can I offer you. When I think about all the events, this is the most welcome news that you have brought me today, which bears no comparison with any I have heard in the world before. Friend forever you have put me in your debt. Now tell me the story of the Lord's doings''. Hanuman bows his head before Bharata's feet and narrates the entire story of Rama's exploits. Bharata asks Hanuman, ''Tell me, does the king Lord ever think of me as his slave''. When Hanuman hears this pitiful question of Bharata, overcome with rapture he falls at the feet of Bharata and says, ''Master, you are dear to Rama as life itself. Friend , I am speaking the truth''. Bharata embraces him repeatedly when he hears this statement. His heart overflows with joy (pp. 823-824).

CONCLUSION

Hanuman's origin as a folk god are traceable from Rgvedic times. His association with Marut and *Vrsakapi* indicate his ancient origins. However, it is difficult to clearly identify the Hanuman who emerged as a god in the *Puranas* with the one who has ancient roots. The*Vrsakapi*, association is particularly important, since *Vrsakapi*, as the name indicates, is regarded as an equal of Indra. Hanuman's identity as a folk god is akin to the Yaksa cult found in the Buddhist literature of 500 B.C. onwards. Also, Hanuman has never been accorded the status of an important god, although he is identified with Rudra and Siva.

Yaksa is a generic term for the folk gods found in the ancient literature of India. *Yaksas* have animal births and other supernatural features which make them important enough to be closed as gods. Perhaps, Hanuman initially was a local folk god worshipped by the people for strength and other attributes leading them to success. It is not without reason, therefore, that Hanuman is a patron god of people engaged in sports and wrestling. The *Ramayana* stresses these Hanuman qualities. He is an expert warrior, lifts mountains with ease, flies and easily kills powerful *raksasas*. The warrior hero displays his heroic strength in his assignments, particularly that of finding Sita. Hanuman, a character subordinate to Rama, in the *Ramayana* of the later periods, is the archetype of the hero who helps others.

In the *Puranas*, Hanuman is a god but of questionable origin. All the birth stories of Hanuman indicate that he is conceived as a child not out of wedlock but through a union between a god and an Apsara. His parents appear very infrequently in the *Ramayana*. This is significant. He has no lineage since he is the product of a union between two divinities. The authors of the *Puranas* are apparently hard pressed to accommodate Hanuman in their scheme. He has to remain a god in their scheme yet he does not deserve a place in the pantheon of gods. He is regarded as an incarnation of Rudra and Siva but no *Purana* of the medieval centuries is named after him.

There are other puzzling aspects of Hanuman in his *Puranic* imagery. He is a *brahmacari* god, a celibate god with a powerful *siddhi*. If Hanuman is considered a yaksa, it is easier to understand this aspect of Hanuman's character. Like a yaksa he is single and like him he is a god of the earth and has power over it. Again, like a yaksa, he is not overburdened with metaphysical pining. In this context it may be recalled that though folk mother goddesses often do not have husbands they do possess power. Kali, Durga and Saraswati are examples. They are not associated with male gods. Hanuman's *brahmacarya* thus offers a male analogy. Hanuman's strength is due to his conserving the *virya*, a quality required of people engaged in purposeful pursuits in Indian tradition. There is, of course, the psychological aspect of Hanuman's *brahmacarya*. Babb's observation that Hanuman's chastity is the result of his chaste devotion to Rama needs consideration. Hanuman's total devotion to Rama, however, rather contributes to *bhakti than brahmacarya.* Flaherty's statement that the power of Hanuman is due to his image of a conserver of seed, is the more likely explanation of Hanuman's *brahmacarya*.

Hanuman in the *Ramayana* and Sanskrit drama evolves into an ideal person. Hanuman is the envoy of Sugriva and King Rama. He displays all the characteristics of an ideal envoy. By his diplomatic skills, he cements an everlasting friendship between Rama and Sugriva. He is archetypal envoy of the *arthasastra*. He not only forges an alliance between the two leaders but also engages in covert operations against Ravana for his new ally Rama. However, unlike the *arthasastra* tradition, he is not the originator of palace plots. He has no evil in him. Sanskrit dramas using Hanuman as the central figure portray Hanuman as a consummate diplomat. It is noteworthy that in his role as an envoy, Hanuman is totally 'human'. His supernatural attributes are not called into play.

As a diplomat, Hanuman is intelligent, learned and shrewdly analyses human emotions. He directs his friends, comrades and allies by teaching them the philosophy of life. His skills as an erudite scholar are really an extension of his role as an envoy of Sugriva and Rama.

Hanuman's heroism is another extraordinary attribute of his personality. Here again he is the ideal one. He is the warrior who accomplishes all impossible tasks. In his role as a warrior hero, Hanuman's folk god image merges with his human image. As a warrior his feats are supernatural : his lifting of the mountain, his airborne activities, his assumption of various forms, his invulnerability to weapons and his single handed battles with the brave *raksasa* warriors. Only a god can accomplish such tasks but Hanuman, out of his loyalty and devotion to his ally and master finds the tasks easy. Valmiki has succecded in blending the human and superhuman qualities in Hanuman in his role as a warrior. His human and superhuman strength and prowess as a warrior beacme a symbol of *sakti* (power). From a simple human being he is transformed into a supreme manifestation of *sakti* who is worshipped for strength and virility.

The powerful warrior is also a model of loyalty and *bhakti*, submitting himself to Rama. This is another extraordinary quality of Hanuman developed in the *Ramayana* and Sanskrit drama. Hanuman is the epitone of the trust and loyalty expected of a servant of the King, an ideal which serves to remind one of feudalism. Hanuman even today is synonymous with loyalty.

Loyalty is easily transformed into love and devotion. The sentiments of *bhakti*, which are well presented in Sanskrit drama, also form the leitmotif of Tulsidas' work. For Tulsidas, Hanuman's *bhakti* to Rama becomes an ideal pattern for socio-religious duties.

Thus, Hanuman, an ideal human being, a loyal and devoted servant and above all a morally upright man, becomes a *bhagwan* (god) for his devotee.

NOTES

Introduction

1. The *rot* is made up of white flour and unrefined sugar (*gud*) which are mixed with water and then made into a ball that is fried in ghee. It is then broken into small pieces.
2. Hanuman Sharma, "Sri Hanuman Ki Upasna", *Kalyana*, year 49, p.486.
3. K.C. Aryan, *Hanuman in Art and Mythology*, (Rekha Prakashan, 1975), p.20.
4. *Ibid.*
5. Dr. Rasmohan Chakravarti, "Bangiya Smriti Avam Tantrik Nibando Mein Hanuman", *Kalyana*, year 49, p. 415.
6. Govind Chandra Rai, *Hanuman ke Devata Tatha Murti Ka Vikas*, Hindi Samelan, Prayag, 1976, pp. 81-89.
7. *Ibid.*
8. G.S. Ghurye, *The Legacy of the Ramayana*, Popular Prakashan, Bombay, 1979.
9. J.N. Banerjee, *The Development of Hindu Iconography*, University of Calcutta, 1956.
10. K.C. Aryan, *Hanuman in Art and Mythology*, Rekha Prakashan, Delhi, 1975.
11. Camil Bulcke, *Rama Katha*, Hindi Parisadha Prakashan, Prayaag, Vishvadyalaya, 1971.
12. Leonard T. Wolcott, " The Power Dispensing Monkey in North Indian Folk Relegion", *The Journal of Asian Studies*, Vol.37, November 1977.
13. See pp. 26-28.
14. G.S. Ghurye, *Gods and Men*, p. 229.
15. Sri Bhau Acharya Tonpe, "Madhava Sampradaya Mein Hanuman", *Kalyana*, year 49, p. 390.
16. The question whether the *vanaras* were a tribe of humans or monkeys is not debated much because the customs, rites, relegions and mannerisms that these *vanaras* followed are all human. (see G.H. Bhatt and U.P. Shah, *V. Ramayana, K.K.*, Introduction, pp. 33, 263, 2). However Valmiki and the other dramatists projecting *vanaras* as monkeys class them as monkeys or humans in accordance with the requirements of the plot. For instance, Rama kills Bali as an animal but coronates his brother Sugriva as a man (See *Abhiseka Nataka* 1. pp. 30-32, *Ramayana*). Sita is surprised to know about the friendship between a monkey and human beings (*Prasanna Hanuman Nataka*, p. 345). When Hanuman praises Laksmana before Sugrive for his high moral character, the latter accepts this fact by giving an argument that they (Rama and Laksmana) behaved so because they are humans but we are *vanaras* (*Prasanna Hanuman Nataka*, 2, p.41).

PART ONE

I. The Origin of Hanuman

1. *Ramayana* of Valmiki, U.K. 19,16 (Critical Edition).
2. *Ibid*, 36,16.
3. *Ibid*, K.K., 65,18.
4. Quoted in Govinda Chandra Rai, *op. cit.*, p.182.
5. *Sumaga Jataka Katha*, Book IX, No. 436.
6. Govinda Chandra Rai, l.s.c.
7. Camile Bulcke, *op.cit.*, p. 655.

8. D.L. Narasimhachar, "The Jaina Ramayana," *Indian Historical Quarterly No. 1*, March 1939, pp. 574-579; V.M. Kulkarni, "Origin and Development of Rama Story in Jaina Literature," Journal of Oriental Institute, Vol. 9, No.3, March 1960, pp. 284-304.
9. *Paumacariyam*, (Jaina), of Vimalasuri translated, (Prakrit Sanskrit Text Society, Varanasi, 1963), 17, 121.
10. *Uttara Purana* (Jaina), of Gunabhadra Pannalal Jain, Jnanapeetha, Kashi, 1954). 68, pp. 278-279.
11. *Padam Purana* (Jaina), of Ravisena (Pannalal Jain Bhartiya Jnanapeetha, Part I, July 1958, Part II, February 1959), 17, pp. 394-397; 18, 122, 124, 409.
12. *Anjana Pavanajaya Nataka*, of Hastimalla (M.V. Patwardhan, Manik Chandra Jain, Digamber Jain Granthamala Samiti, Heerabaga, Mumbapuri-4), I, p. 2.
13. *Padam Purana, op.cit.*, 19, p. 415.
14. *Narasimha Purana*, ed. Udhavacharya, 2nd ed., (Gopal Narayan Company, Kalbadevi Road), 47, 33, 35; 52, 112
15. *Visnudharmotra Purana*, Gaikwad Oriental Series, Baroda, 1958.
16. *Skanda Purana, Vaisnava Khanda*, (Naval Kishor Press), Pt. 2, 39:8: 39:45.
17. *Skanda Purana, Avanti Khanda*, 79, 5, 6.
18. *Bhavisya Purana, Pratisarga Parva Khanda*, (Khemraj, Venkateshwara Press, Mumbai),4, 13, 32, 33.
19. *Ibid*, 4, 40-42.
20. *Brahma vaivarta Purana, Krishna Janma Khanda*, (Moar Samskarna) Calcutta,1955), 62, 62.
21. *Mahabhagavata Purana*, Ch. 37, Also see , Bulcke p. 661.
22. *Brhaddharma Purana, Purva Khanda*, (Asiatic Society of Bengal and Calcutta, 1895), 18, 38.
23. *Ibid*, 20, 34-36.
24. *Siva Maha Purana, Satarudra Samhita* (Pandit Jwala Prasad Mishra, Venkateshwara Mudralaya, Bombay), 20, 4, 5, 6.
25. *Ibid*, 20, Kapitanu (20:7), Kapisan (20:8), Kapivara (20:14), Kapi Kunjara (20:16), Hanuman Vanesavera (20:17), Kapi Nayak (20:20) and Kapisavara (20:18). In the *Ramayana*, he is called by the synonyms of Simadivarga, 3). *vanara*. In the *Amar Kosa* nine synonyms of *vanaras* are mentioned *Amarkosa*. He is called Hari also (*Amarkosa, Kanda, Nana Artha Varga*, 175).
26. *Siva Maha Purana op. cit.*, 20, 17.
27. D.S. Fucas, *The Gond and Bhumiya of Eastern Mandala*, Bombay 1960, pp. 421-422. See also *Asiatic Research*, Part II, p. 141; Indian Antiquary, Part II, p. 229; W. Crooks, *Tribes and Castes*, Part I, p. 269; H.A. Ross, *A Glossary of the Tribes and Castes*, Part II, p. 391.
28. *Siva Purana, Mahesvara Mahatmya*, Kedar Nath Khanda, 8,99-100.
29. *Visnudharmotra Purana*, I, 222, 7-8.
30. *Narada Purana, Trtaya Pada*, 78, 20, 24-25.
31. *Brahma Purana, Pesacatiratha Mahtmya*, (Anandashram Sanskrit Granthawali 28), 18, 12.
32. *Ibid* 18, 18,
33. *Ananda Ramayana, Sara Kanda*, (Moolgavankar, Gopal Narayan Company, Bombay, 1926), 1, 107.
34. *Ibid.* 13.162-163; E. Moor narrates the same story with little variation. *Pavana* or *Vayu* commissions a Marut, one of the attendent gods, to watch for *Payasa* falling from the dragonfly's beak and to hand it over to Anjana. The obedient Marut does as he is told. Hanuman thus acquires the name Marut, the son of Marut. *The Hindu Pantheon*, (London,

1910), p. 316. See also C. Colemn, *The Mythology of Hindus*, (London, 1932), pp. 57-58.

35. *Ananda Ramayana, Sara Kanda*, 1, 12, 147-149.
36. *Ibid., Manohar Kanda*, Sarga 13.
37. *Ibid., Manohar Kanda*, Sarga 16.
38. *Ibid., Sara Kanda*, 12, 147-149.
39. *Ibid., Sara Kanda*, 10, 143-144.
40. *Anjana Pavanajaya Nataka*, 7,12; 8, p.115.
41. *Amargha Raghava Nataka* of Murari, 5, 51 (Niryana Sagar Press, Bombay, 1909), 5, 51.
42. *Hanuman Nataka* of Damodar Mishra, (Chowkamba Sanskrit Series Office, Varanasi, 1976), 6, 27.
43. *Ibid.*

II Hanuman as Ciranjiva (Immortal)

1. *V. Ramayana*, of Valmiki, *K.K.*, 65, 26.
2. *Ibid., U.K.*, 39, 16, 19.
3. *Adhyatama Ramayana*, (Geeta Press, Gorakhpur) 6, 16, 10-14, 142.
4. *Maha Nataka*, Visveswara Dayala, 9, 146, *Prasanna Hanuman Nataka*, (Veralokapura, Itwah), 5, 313.
5. *Mahabharata, Vanaparva*, 275, 43.
6. *Skanda Purana, Avanti Khanda, Chatursitilingam*, 79, 35-36.
7. *Visnudharmotra Purana*, 1-223, 26-35.
8. Govinda Chandra Rai *op. cit.*, p.294.
9. In the *Upnisadas*, Vayu appears as the cosmic life breath. The *Mahabharata* (12:328,25) calls him the life breath of the world, the universal spirit, the impeller of life and of the living.

III Aryan and Dravidian Origins of Hanuman

1. *Rgveda*, 10.86.1.
2. H.D. Velankar, "Hymns to Indra in Mandala 10", *Journal of the University of Bombay*, September 1953, p. 14.
3. F.E. Pargitar, " Vrsakapi And Hanuman", *Journal of the Royal Asiatic society*, 1913, p.400.
4. F.E. Pargitar, " Suggestion Regarding Rgveda 10-68, " *Journal of the Royal Asiatic Society*, 1911. pp. 803, 808.
5. *Ibid*, p. 809.
6. F.E. Pargitar, "Vrsakapi and Hanumant, *op. cit.*, p. 397.
7. *Ibid.*, pp. 399-400. The Aryans, when they Sanskritised Dravidian words, sometimes converted the first *deergha* (long) into *hrva* (short) and sometimes added the prefix ha to it. In this way Anmandi became Anmand, then Hanmandi, Hanmanti and finally Hanumant. Pargitar argues that Hidimba in the *Mahabharta* (1.152) was Idumbi (In Tamil it means hot-tempered women). When Sanskritised, it became Hidimba. In the *Uttara Purana* of Gunabhadra, Anmant became Hanuman.
8. Govinda Chandra Rai, *op. cit.*, p. 18
9. F.E. Pargitar, "Vrsakapi and Hanumant", *op. cit.*, pp. 396-397
10. S.K. Chatterji, *The Vedic Age*, (Bhartiya Vidya Mandir, Bombay), p. 164.
11. G.S. Ghurye, *Gods and Men*, (Popular Book Depot, Bombay), p. 226.
12. *Ibid.*

IV Hanuman as Yaksa

1. Vasudeva Sharan Aggarwala. *Prachina Bhartiya Loka Dharma*, (Jnanodaya Trust , Ahmdabad 1964) p. 133.
2. *Sindur* also symbolises the sacrifice of animals offered in tree worship. The folk deities fit to be painted red with sindur and to receive non-vegetarian offerings. (Gunther D. Sotheimer, Heidelberg, "Folk Deities in the Vijayanagar Empire, Narsimha and Mallana Maiter," in *Vijayanagar City and Empire. New Currents of Research*, Anna Libero Dalla Piccolo in collaboration with Stephanie Zingel-Ave-Lallemant, Steiner Verlag Weisbaden Gmbh, Stuttgart, 1985) p. 145.
3. *Ibid.*
4. J.N.Bannerjee, *The Development of Hindu Iconography*,p. 349.
5. A.K. Coomarswami,*Yaksas*,(Munshi Manohar Lal, New Delhi,1971) Part I, p.7.
6. A.K. Coomarswami, *op. cit.*, p.18 and J.N. Bannerjee, *op. cit.*, p. 341.
7. Govinda Chandra Rai, *op. cit.*, p. 366.
8. W.Crooke, Encyclopaedia of Religion and Ethnics, Part 2, Bengal.
9. *The Tribes of Madhya Pradesh* (Department of Tribal Welfare, Govenment of M.P. Bhopal, 1964), pp. 15-17.
10. W. Crooke, *The Tribes and Castes of North Western Provinces of Oudh*, (Calcutta, 1896) Part I, pp. 193, 203, 215

V Hanuman Worship and his Attributes in Modern India

1. Leonard T. Wolcott, *op. cit.*, p. 656.
2. Dr. Manohar Sharma, "Rajasthani Lok Sahitya Mein Mahavira Hanuman, "*Kalyana*, Year 49, pp. 469-470.
3. Sushil Kumar, "Adivasi Lok Jeewan Mein Sri Hanumanji", *Kalyana*, year 49, p. 478.
4. G.S. Ghurye, *Gods and Men, op. cit.*, p.236.
5. *Ramayana*, of Tulsidas, translated by S.P. Bahadur, (Prachya Prakashan, Varanasi, 1979) *Lanka Kanda*, 7, 8, 16.
6. Leonard T. Wolcott, *op. cit.*, p. 658.
7. *Ibid.*
8. Rama Vallabha Pandey, " Bundeli Lok Sahitya Mein Hanuman, " *Kalyana*, year 49, pp. 474-475.
9. Leonard T. Wolcott, *op. cit.*, p. 659.
10. Quoted in a Camile Bulcke, *Ramakatha, op. cit.*, p. 684.
11. *Ibid.* p.685.
12. Govind Chandra Rai, *Hanuman*, etc., *op. cit.*, p.86.
13. *Ibid.*, p. 87.

VI Hanuman As *Brahmacari*

1. *Ananda Ramayana, Manohara Kanda*, Sarga 13, *op. cit.*.
2. Madhava Chingle, "Smarth Sampradaya," *Kalyana*, year 49, p.167.
3. *Bhavartha Ramayana*, 7, 35; 4, 10. C. Bulcke, *Ramakatha*, p. 679; In *Padam Purana, Patala Khanda*, 112, 135, Hanuman is called *Sudrabadh Mounji Kaupina* (Ananda Ashram Sanskrit Grantha mala-131, Vishvanath Narayana Mandlya, Poona, 1894). According to the Oriya Mahabharata of Sarladasa, Hanuman told his mother that he would not be born unless he would get *Vajrakaupina*, Pavana sent his message to Siva and Siva gave Anjana clothes to eat. This resulted in Anjana giving birth to Hanuman

with *Kaupina* on him (See Bulcke *op. cit.*, pp. 678-679). There is another folk tale narrated by M.A. Macalliffe that Hanuman robbed a *rsi* of everything, leaving only his *Kaupina* on him. The angry *rsi*, cursing him said, " You will have nothing on your body except *kaupina*. You won't be able to wear anything else" (*The Sikh Religion*, Clarendon Press, 1909, Part 6, p. 82).

4. *Padam Purana* (Hindu), *Patala Khanda*, 45, 31; Govinda Chandra Rai, *Hanuman*, etc, *op. cit.*, p. 295
5. *Ramayana*, of Valmiki, *Sundara-Kanda*, 9, 35.
6. *Ibid*, 9, 38, 39.
7. Lawrence A.Babb, *The Divine Hierarchy*, (Popular Hinduism in Central India, Columbia University Press, New York, 1975), p. 233.
8. W.D.O'Flaherty, *Ascetcism and Eroticism in the Mythology of Siva*, (London, Oxford University Press, New York, 1973), p. 262
9. Lawrence A. Babb *op. cit.*, p. 232.
10. *Skanda Purana, Avanti Khanda op. cit.*, 83, 33.
11. *Paumacariyam*, Sarga 52, Bulcke *op. cit.*, p. 497; *Padam Purana* (Jaina), *op. cit.*, and Govinda Chandra Rai, *Hanuman*, etc., *op. cit.*, p. 296
12. *Paumacariyam*, 19, 32, 24-37, 41 & 42.
13. *Paumacariyam*, Sarga 52 *op. cit.*, and Bulcke *op. cit.*, p. 497.
14. *Ramayana, of Valmiki*, 113, 41.
15. *Adhyatama Ramayana*, Y.K., Sarga 14, 60-61.
16. *Ananda Ramayana, Sarakanda*, 11, 86-90.
17. *Prasanna Hanuman Nataka*, 5, *op. cit.*, p.102 and 104.
18. Bulcke, *op. cit.*, p. 679.
19. *Seri Rama Katha*, in Bulcke, *op. cit.*, 679.

PART TWO

I Hanuman in Sanskrit Drama

1. *Hanuman Nataka*, 6, p.12 and Ramayana, of Valmiki, K.K.,43, 4.
2. *Hanuman Nataka*, 6, p. 96 and Ramayana, of Valmiki, K.K., 43, 2, 4.
3. Vishvanath, *Saugandhi Ka Harana Nataka*, (Chowkhambha Vidya Bhawan Chowk, Varanasi,1963), p. 27.
4. *Ibid.* and *Ramayana*, of Valmiki, *K.K.*, 43, 6, 13; 65, 25 & 27.
5. *Prasanna Hanuman Nataka*, 2, p. 50. Ramayana, of Valmiki, K.K., 66.1.
6. *Prasanna Hanuman Nataka*, p. 50.
7. *Ibid.*
8. *Ibid*, p.89 and *Ramayana*, of Valmiki, *K.K.*, 43, 2, 4, 5, 6; 65. 3.5.6; 66, 6.
9. *Ibid*, 65, 18.
10. *Ibid, U.K.*, 35-42.
11. *Prasanna Hanuman Nataka*, 1, 21.
12. *Ibid.*, 1,32 and *Saugandhi Ka Harana Nataka*, p. 29.
13. Bhavabhuti, *Mahavira Caritam Nataka*, (Chowkhamba Vidya Bhawan, Varanasi, 1960), 5, 31.
14. *Anargha Raghava Nataka*, 5, 51.
15. *Prasanna Hanuman Nataka*, 3, 204, 205, *Hanuman Nataka*,7,5, Ramayana, of Valmiki, K.K., 43, 1, 2-5; 8, 13 and S.K., 1, 180.
16. *Prasanna Hanuman Nataka*, p. 43.
17. *Ibid* 2, 155 and Ramayana, of Valmiki, *K.K.*, 65, 36; 66, 44.

18.*Prasanna Hanuman Nataka*, 2, 155.
19.*Anargha Raghava Nataka*, 5, 51.
20.*Prasanna Hanuman Nataka*, 2, 155.
21.*Hanuman Nataka*, 6, 2 and 4.
22.*Prasanna Hanuman Nataka*, 2, 155.
23.*Ramayana*, of Valmiki, *S.K.*, 1, 118, 119.
24.*Hanuman Nataka*, 6, 11.
25.*Prasanna Hanuman* Nataka, 2, 160 and *Maha Nataka*, 5, 37.
26.*Ramayana*, of Valmiki, *S.K.*, 1, 133.
27.Bhasa, *Abhiseka Nataka*, (Motilal Banarasidas, Varanasi) 2, 22.
Saktibhadra, *Ascarya Cudamini Nataka*, (Chowkambha, Vidyabhawan, Varanasi, 1966) 6,1, Someswara, *Ullagha Raghava Nataka*, (Gaekwad's Oriental Series No. 132, Oriental Institute, Baroda, 1961) 6, 3 and *Janaki Parineya Nataka*, 7, p.194.
28.*Prasanna Hanuman Nataka*, 3, p. 53.
29.*Ibid.*, p.63. and *Ramayana*, of Valmiki, *S.K.*, 1, 179.
30.*Abhiseka Nataka*, 3, 1.
31.*Ramayana*, of Valmiki, *S.K.* 39, 4, 8, 10, 11, 12.
32.*Abhiseka Nataka*, 3.1.
33.*Ibid* 3, pp. 88, 89.
34.*Prasanna Hanuman Nataka*, 3, p. 60.
35.*Abhiseka Nataka*, 3, 7.
36.*Prasanna Hanuman Nataka*, 6, p. 337.
37.*Hanuman Nataka*, 8, 9; 14, 61.
38.*Ibid.*, 14, 1.
39.*Prasanna Hanuman Nataka*, 6, p. 325.
40.*Ibid*, 3, p. 62.
41.*Ibid*, 3, p. 63.
42.*Abhiseka Nataka*, 3, 16.
43.*Ramayana*, of Valmiki, *S.K.* 50, 6, 7.
44.*Ibid.*, 51, 12-13.
45.*Mahavira Caritam Nataka*, 6, 4, 5, and *Hanuman Nataka*, 6, 25, and *Anargha Raghava Nataka*, 6, 1 and 2.
46.*Prasanna Hanuman Nataka*, 3, pp. 191-193.
47.*Janaki Parinaya Nataka*, 6, 72.
48.*Hanuman Nataka*, 8, 6.
49.*Ibid.*, 8, 9.
50.*Ibid.*, 11, 36, 38.
51.*Prasanna Hanuman Nataka*, 4, p. 84, *Mahavira Caritam Nataka*, 6, p. 285 and *Ullagha Raghava Nataka*, 7, 4.
52.*Ramayana*, of Valmiki, *Y.K.*, 55, 124, 125.
53.*Ibid.*, 64, 16, 17, 22, 23.
54.*Janaki Parinaya Nataka*, 7, p. 185.
55.*Ramayana*, of Valmiki, *Y.K.*, 58-40.
56.*Hanuman Nataka*, 14, 4.
57.*Saugandhi ka Haran Nataka*, 1, 74.
58.*Ibid.*, 1, 62.
59.*Ullagha Raghava Nataka*, 6, p. 113.
60.*Ramayana*, of Valmiki, *Y.K.*, 47, 62-63.
61.*Ibid.*, Y.K., 69, 70.
62.*Ibid.*, Y.K., 47, 108-110.
63.*Anargha Raghava Nataka*, 6, p. 365.

64. *Hanuman Nataka,* 13, 1.
65. *Ibid.,*
66. *Ibid.,* 13, 6.
67. *Ibid.,*
68. *Ibid.,* 13, 17.
69. *Ibid.,* 13, 209.
70. *Prasanna Hanuman Nataka,* 7, 33, *Ullagha Raghava Nataka,* 7, pp. 127-128 and *Mahavira Caritam Nataka,* 6, p. 287.
71. *Prasanna Hanuman Nataka,* 4, p. 90; Griffiths mentions another variation of the episode. Kalanemi, Ravana's uncle, is promised half of Ravana's kingdom if he eliminates Hanuman. Kalanemi disguises himself as a devotee of Rama and invites Hanuman to share a meal with him. Hanuman declines the offer. (R.T.H. Griffiths, *The Ramayana of Valmiki,* (Banaras, 1915, p. 275).
72. *Prasanna Hanuman Nataka,* 4, p. 90.
73. *Ibid.*
74. *Ibid.,* 4, p. 11.
75. *Hanuman Nataka,* 13, 32.
76. *Ibid.,* 13, 23.
77. *Prasanna Hanuman Nataka,* 4, p. 89.
78. *Ramayana,* of Valmiki, 61, 58.
79. *Prasanna Hanuman Nataka,* 4, p. 92.
80. *Hanuman Nataka,* 13, 27.
81. *Ibid.,* 13, 20.
82. *Saugandhi Ka Harana Nataka,* 4, p. 49.
83. The episode in the *Mahabharata* mentions that Bhima tried to lift Hanuman's tail with his club so that he might cross the path that Hanuman was resting upon. Unable to accomplish this, it occurred to Bhima that Hanuman might not be an ordinary ape. Bhima apologised for his behaviour and requested that Hanuman reveal his identity to him. On Bhima's request, Hanuman showed him the form that he had assumed when he jumped over the ocean to Lanka. (*Mahabharata, Vanaparva,* 147, 13, 20, 21).
84. *Mahavira Caritam Nataka,* 6, 40.
85. *Hanuman Nataka,* 14, p. 219.
86. According to the *Mahabharata,* Hanuman told Bhima that he would be at the flag of Arjuna during the battle of *Mahabharata.* He would make a terrible, deafening roar that would terrorise the enemy, making the battle easy to win. (*Mahabharata, Vanaparva,* 150, 14-15) See Tulsidas, *Vinaya Patrika,* (Chowkhamba Sanskrit Series, Prachya Prakashan, Varanasi) 28, 3.
87. In the *Ananda Ramayana,* Visnudasa asks Ramadasa the reason why Arjun's flag is called *kapidhavaja.* Ramadasa, answering this question, narrates this story: Hanuman tells Bhima that if he made the *Sara Setu,* it wouldn't be strong enough to bear his mighty weight and would have possibly sunk into the sea. Arjuna heard this and decided to take a bet with Hanuman, "I will make the *Sara Setu,*" he said. "If it sinks into the sea due to your weight I will enter a blaze of fire." Hanuman agreed and promised that if *Sara Setu* did not sink with the touch of his toe, he would stand by Arjuna's flag. Arjuna built the bridge and Hanuman, with the touch of his toe, sank it. Arjuna was about to fulfill his promise of walking into a blazing fire when Krsna appeared in disguise and said that without any witnesses there bet was invalid. He asked them to repeat the events of the bet.. Before Hanuman placed his toe on a newly built bridge, Krsna put his *cakra* under the bridge to prevent it from sinking. Hanuman immediately recognised Krsna disguised as a brahman. Krsna assumed his natural form and embraced Hanuman. Krsna saved Arjuna's pride but Hanuman, on account of his commitment to Arjuna, sat at Arjuna's flag

since that day. (*Ananda Ramayana, Manohara Kanda*, 18, 21, 22).
88. *Mahavira Caritam Nataka*, 6, p. 279.
89. *Saughandika Harana Nataka*, 1, 54 and 64.
90. *Hanuman Nataka*, 14, 3.
91. *Ananda Ramayana*, 8, 123.

II HANUMAN AS POLITICIAN AND MILITARY COMMANDER

1. *Ramayana*, of Valmiki, *K.K.*, 5, 14, 15.
2. *Hanuman Nataka*, 5, 39.
3. *Janaki Parinaya Nataka*, 6, 54, and *Prasanna Hanuman Nataka*, 1, 54.
4. *Anargha Raghava Nataka*, 5, p. 292.
5. *Ibid.*, pp. 298-299.
6. *Hanuman Nataka*, 14, 62.
7. *Prasanna Hanuman Nataka*, 1, 43, 44, 46.
8. *Ibid.*, 1, pp. 21-22.
9. *Anargha Raghava Nataka*, 5, 51.
10. *Adbhuta Darpana Nataka*, 1, p. 6 and *Anargha Raghava Nataka*, 6, p. 332.
11. *Ramayana*, of Valmiki, *S.K.*, 15, 23, 24.
12. *Abhiseka Nataka*, 2, 59.
13. *Hanuman Nataka*, 6, 13.
14. *Abhisheka Nataka*, p. 101, verse 15 and *Ramayana*, of Valmiki, *S.K.*, 49, 2, 3.
15. *Prasanna Hanuman Nataka*, 3, pp. 186-188 and *Ramayana*, of Valmiki, *U.K.*, 11, 21.
16. *Hanuman Nataka*, 6, 22.
17. *Abhiseka Nataka*, p. 101, verse 15.
18. *Abhiseka Nataka*, 3, 23 and *Ramayana*, of Valmiki, 49, 34, 35.
19. *Prasanna Hanuman Nataka*, 2, 133 and *Hanuman Nataka*, 6, 7. According to Navalkara, Hanuman was entrusted with two vital tasks. If he succeeded it would be plain sailing to victory, if he failed, victory would be despaired of. The first task was to discover a passage across the channel for conveying large body of troops easily and quickly to the shore of Lanka; unless such a passage was discovered, further movement would come to a standstill. See Navalkara, *A New Approach to the Ramayana*, p. 190.
20. *Ramayana*, of Valmiki, *Y.K.*, 3, 8 and 27.
21. *Ibid.*, *S.K.*, 41, 34, 35, 36.
22. *Abhiseka Nataka*, 3, 83, 84.
23. *Ibid.*, 2, 26.
24. *Ibid.*, 3, 14.
25. *Ibid.*, 3, 11.
26. *Ramayana*, of Valmiki, *S.K.*, 51, 13 and 14.
27. *Ibid.*
28. *Ibid.*, *Y.K.*, 3, 28, 30.
29. *Maha Nataka*, 6, 69
30. *Prasanna Hanuman Nataka*, 2, p. 32, and *Hanuman Nataka*, 7, 1.
31. *Ramayana*, of Valmiki, *Y.K.*, 11, 57, 58.
32. *Abhiseka Nataka*, 4, 9, 10.
33. *Prasanna Hanuman Nataka*, 4, p. 227.
34. *Anargha Raghava Nataka*, 5, p. 314.
35. *Abhiseka Nataka*, 4, pp. 138, 139 and *Ramayana*, of Valmiki, Y.K., 4, 7.
36. *Prasanna Hanuman Nataka*, 2, p. 32.
37. *Hanuman Nataka*, 12, 18.

38. *Abhiseka Nataka*, 2, 16; 2, pp. 71, 80; 3, 14 and *Prasanna Hanuman Nataka*, 3, pp. 62, 351.
39. *Ramayana*, of Valmiki, *K.K.*, 43, 6.
40. *Ibid.*, 28, 6.

III Hanuman's Intellectual Achievements

1. *Samyutta Nikaya*, (Pali Text Society, London, 1884), Vol. I, p. 206.
2. *Samyutta Nikaya*, pp. 207, 213.
3. Rama Nath Mishra, *Yaksa Cult and Iconography*, p. 24.
4. *Ramayana*, of Valmiki, *K.K.*, 28; 7.
5. *Ibid.*, *K.K.*, 65, 18.
6. *Ibid.*, *K.K.*, 43, 6.
7. *Ibid.*, *U.K.*, 36, 14.
8. *Ibid.*, *K.K.*, 43, 6.
9. *Ibid.*, *K.K.*, 65, 2. Tulsidas calls him *Ved Vedanta-vid* (One who knows *Veda*) (*Vinaya Patrika* 23, 8), Geeta Press, Gorakhpur.
10. *Mahabharata*, *Vanaparva*, 148, 9, 39.
11. *Ramayana*, of Valmiki, *U.K.*, 36, 42.
12. *Saugandhi Ka Harana Nataka*, p. 43.
13. *Ramayana*, of Valmiki, *S.K.*, 28, 17, 18.
14. *Abhiseka Nataka*, 2, 16, p. 71, *Saugandhi Ka Harana Nataka*, pp. 20-22 and *Prasanna Hanuman Nataka*, 2, 73, 74.
15. *Hanuman Nataka*, 6, 15.
16. *Ramayana*, of Valmiki, *Y.K.*, 11, 57, 58.
17. *Ibid.*, *S.K.*, 2, 23, 24, 27.
18. *Saugandhi Ka Harana Nataka*, pp. 20-22.
19. *Ramayana*, of Valmiki, *K.K.*, 3, 25.
20. *Ascarya Cudamani Nataka*, 6, 16, 7.
21. *Prasanna Hanuman Nataka*, 1, 43, 44.
22. *Abhiseka Nataka*, 2, p. 71, 79 and *Prasanna Hanuman Nataka*, p. 65.
23. *Ascarya Cudamani Nataka*, 6, 6 and *Prasanna Hanuman Nataka*, 3, p. 59.
24. *Prasanna Hanuman Nataka*, 2, p. 49.
25. *Abhiseka Nataka*, 3, p. 101.
26. *Abhiseka Nataka*, 2, 7.
27. *Ibid.*, 2, 8.
28. *Ramayana*, of Valmiki, *S.K.*, 13, 31, 32.
29. *Ibid.*, 13, 32, 33, 36, 37.
30. *Hanuman Nataka*, 13; 23.
31. *Prasanna Hanuman Nataka*, 4, p. 91.
32. *Saugandhi Ka Harana Nataka*, 1, 21. Tulsidas calls Hanuman *fana guna garva gandh arvajeta, Sama gayaka, Sama gana agrani*, (*Vinaya Patrika*, 29-4; 28-5; 27-3) Geeta Press, Gorakhpur.
33. *Mahabharata*, *Vanaparva*, 147, 39.
34. Cited in Braj Kishor Prasad, "Sangeeta Acharya Hanuman", *Kalyana*, year 49, p. 388.
35. *Ibid.*, p. 389.
36. Cited in Dinesh Chandra, *Bengali Ramayana*, p. 51.
37. Cited in Shiva Shankar Awasthi, "Sangeeta Sastara Mein Hanuman", *Kalyana*, year 49, p. 386.
38. *Ibid.*, p. 387.

39. *Ibid.*
40. *Ibid.*
41. *Ibid.*, p. 386.
42. *Saugandhi Ka Harana Nataka*, pp. 47, 49.
43. *Mahabharata, Aranyaka parva*, 146, 40, 41.
44. *Saugandhi Ka Harana Nataka*, 93, p. 48.
45. *Skanda Purana, Brahma Kanda, Dharmayan Mahatmaya*, 37, 18.
46. *Hanuman Nataka*, 13, 13, 14.
47. *Ibid.*, 1, p.19.
48. *Ramayana*, of Valmiki, *K.K.*, 21, 2, 3.
49. *Prasanna Hanuman Nataka*, 2, 73, 74.
50. K.C. Aryan, "The Hanuman Cult", *Illustrated Weekly of India*, March 1976, p. 26.

IV Hanuman's Rama *Bhakti*

1. Herman Jacobi, *Das Ramayana*, pp. 50-51.
2. *Ramayana*, of Valmiki, *U.K.*, 39, 15.
3. *Hanuman Nataka*, 6, 5. In the *Maha Nataka* such an assurance for accomplishing this task is given by Sugriva. (*Maha Nataka*, 6, 24).
4. *Hanuman Nataka*, 5, 39 and *Prasanna Hanuman Nataka*, 1, 54.
5. *Prasanna Hanuman Nataka*, 2, 52.
6. *Ascarya Cudamani Nataka*, 6, p. 186.
7. *Prasanna Hanuman Nataka*, 2, p. 46.
8. *Ibid.*, 4, p. 62.
9. *Hanuman Nataka*, 13, p. 207.
10. *Prasanna Hanuman Nataka*, 4, p. 266.
11. *Hanuman Nataka*, 13, 20.
12. *Ullagha Raghava Nataka*, 7, 14.
13. *Hanuman Nataka*, 7, 19. In the *Maha Nataka*, Vibhisana also shows his devotion towards Rama, by expressing similar feelings.
14. *Ascarya Cudamani Nataka*, 6, 12.
15. *Ibid.*, 6, 11.
16. *Abhiseka Nataka*, 2, p. 59.
17. *Ascarya Cudamani Nataka*, 6, 12 and *Ramayana*, of Valmiki, *S.K.*, 28, 39, 40.
18. *Ascarya Cudamani Nataka*, 6, 12.
19. *Hanuman Nataka*, 6, 20 and *Anargha Raghava Nataka*, 6, 47.
20. *Abhiseka Nataka*, 2, 15.
21. *Ibid.*, 3, 21.
22. *Ramayana*, of Valmiki, *S.K.*, 36, 9.
23. *Prasanna Hanuman Nataka*, 3, p. 54.
24. *Ascarya Cudamani Nataka*, 6, 6.
25. *Ibid.*, 8, pp. 239-241.
26. *Abhiseka Nataka*, 6, p. 204.
27. *Ullagha Raghava Nataka*, 7, 32.
28. *Ramayana*, of Valmiki, *Y.K.*, 113, 26-28.
29. *Ibid.*, 101, 17, 18.
30. *Saugandhi Ka Harana Nataka*, 1, 22.
31. *Prasanna Hanuman Nataka*, 1, 22.
32. *Dutangada Nataka*, 27 and *Hanuman Nataka*, 11, 7.
33. *Prasanna Hanuman Nataka*, 5, p. 114.

34.*Anargha Raghava Nataka*, 6, p. 349.
35.*Mahavira Caritam Nataka*, 7, 30.
36.*Prasanna Hanuman Nataka*, 5, p. 113.
37.*Hanuman Nataka*, 6, 36.
38.*Ibid.*, 7, 19.
39.*Prasanna Hanuman Nataka*, 1, p. 22.
40.*Ibid.*, 2, 52: 3, p. 62.
41.The two versions called *Maha Nataka* and *Hanuman Nataka*. The Damodar Mishra redaction has 548 verses in 14 acts and is called the *Hanuman Nataka* while the Bengal or East Indian redaction arranged by Madhusudana Mishra has 720 verses in 9 acts and is named *Maha Nataka*.
42.*Racitam aniputrentha Valmikinabdhu*
Nihitam Amrta-buddhya pran mahanatakam yat.
Sumati-nrpati bhojenoddhrtan yat Kramena
grathitam avatu visvam misra-damodarena.
(*Hanuman Nataka*, 14, 96)
43.*Atreyam katha-purvam etena nakharo-tankair giri-silasu vilikhitam tat tu Valmikina trstam/tad etasyati-madhuratvam akarnya ramayana pracarabhava-sankaya-hanuman practhitas tuam etat Sam udre nidehiti/tatheti tenabdhav prapitam tadava tarena bhjena Sumatina Jala-jnanair uddhrtam iti.* (*Hanuman -Nataka*, Introduction, P XI)
44.*Kalyana Saugandhi Ka Nataka, Kalyana*, year 49, p. 383.
45.*Rama Carita Manas, Lanka Kanda*, 56, 4-6, Geeta Press, Gorakhpur.
46.*Rama Carita Manas, U.K.*, Part I, translated by S.P. Bahadur, Chowkhamba Sanskrit series, Prachya Prakashan, Varanasi, 1979.
47. *Ananda Ramayana, Sara Kanda*, 12, 143.
48. *Saugandhi Ka Haran Nataka*, 1, 90.
49.*Hanuman Nataka*, 13, 35, 36, *Maha Nataka*, 6, 21, 22 and *Ramayana*, of Valmiki, *Y.K.*, 11, 12.
50.*Maha Nataka*, 6, 8.
51.*Abhiseka Nataka*, 3, 21.
52.*Hanuman Nataka*, 14, 80-81, 83-84.
53.*Bhavisya Purana, Pratisargaparva Khanda*, 4, ch. 13, 46-47.
54.*Kurma Purana, Purva Khanda*, 21, 35.
55.*Siva Maha Purana, Satarudra Samhita*, ch. 20, 20, 36.
56.*Ananda Ramayana, Sara Kanda*, 13, 177-178.
57.*Adhyatama Ramayana*, 16, 12-13, Geeta Press.
58.Cited in C.Bulcke, *Rama Katha*, p. 675.
59.*Ibid.*
60.*Ibid.*
61.*Ibid.*, p. 182.
62.Sri Vedehikanta Sharan, "Ramananda Sampradaya Mein Hanuman," *Kalyana*, year 49, p. 397.

BIBLIOGRAPHY

I. Original Language Texts

Abhiseka Nataka, of Bhasa, Motilal Banarasidas, Chowk Varanasi (n.d.).

Adbhuta Darpana Nataka of Mahadeva, ed., Shivaram Tukaram Javaji, Nirnaya Sagar Press, Bombay (n.d.).

Adhyatma Ramayana, Geeta Press, Gorakhpur (n.d.).

Ananda Ramayana, D.V. Mulgavankar, Gopal Narayana Company, Bombay, 1926.

Anargha Raghava Nataka, of Murari, Nirnaya Sagar Press, Bombay, 1909.

Anjana Pavanjaya Nataka, of Hastimalla, Manik Chander Digamber Jain Granth Mala, Pushpa-13 (n.d.).

Ascarya Cudamani Nataka of Saktibhadra, Chowkhamba Vidya Bhavan, Varanasi, 1966.

Bala Ramayana Nataka, of Rajasekhar, Jiwanand Vidyasagar, 1952.

Bhavisya Purana, Khemraj Sri Krishnadasa, Venkateshwara Press (n.d.)

Brahma Purana, Mansukh Rai Moar, Calcutta, 1954.

Brahma Vaivarta Purana, Asiatic Society of Bengal and Calcutta 1895.

Dutangada Nataka, of Subhata, Chowkhamba Sanskrit Series, Vidya Vilas Press, Varanasi 1950.

Hanuman Nataka, Chowkhamba Sanskrit Series, Varanasi, 1967.

Janaki Parinaya Nataka, of Rambhadra Dikshit (n.d.).

Mahabharata, Poona edition, 1933-1959.

Maha Nataka, of Damodra Mishra, (n.d.).

Mahabhagavata Purana, Geeta Press, Gorakhpur, (n.d.).

Mahavira Caritam Nataka, of Bhavabhuti, Chowkhmaba Vidya bhawan, Varanasi, 1960.

Narasimha Purana, ed. Uddhavacarya, 2nd ed., Gopal Narayana Company, Bombay, 1911.

Narada Purana, Khemraj Sri Krishanadasa, Sri Venkateshwara Press, Mumbai (n.d.).

Padam Purana (Jain), of Ravisenacarya, Bharatiya Jnana Peeth, Part I, July 1958 and Part 2, February 1959

Padam Purana (Hindu), Anandashram Sanskrit Granthamala 131, Visvanath Narayana Mandalika, Poona, 1894.

Prasanna Hanuman Nataka, of Visveswar Dayal, Verlokapura, Itawah, 1944.

Prasanna Raghava Nataka, of Jayadeva, Chowkhamba Vidya Bhawan, Varanasi, 1972.

Rama Carita Manas , of Tulsidas, Geeta Press, Gorakhpur.

Rama Carita Manas , of Tulsidas, Ramayana Press, Bombay, 1987.

Ramayana, of Valmiki, *Bala Kanda*, ed. G.H. Bhatt, Baroda, 1960.

Kiskindha Kanda, ed. D.R. Mankad, 1965; *Sundara Kanda,* ed. G.C. Jhala, 1966; *Yuddha Kanda*, ed. P.L. Vaidya, 1967-71 and Uttara Kanda, ed. P.L. Vaidya 1973-75.

Saugandhi Ka Harana Nataka, of Visvanath, Chowkhamba Vidyabhavan, Varanasi, 1963.

Siva Maha Purana, Pandit Jwala Prasad Mishra, Sri Venkateshwara Mudralaya, Bombay (n.d.).

Skanda Purana, Naval Kishore Press (n.d.)

Ullagha Raghava Nataka, of Someswar, Gaikwad Oriental Series No. 132, Oriental Institute, Baroda, 1961.

Uttara Purana, of Gunabhadra, Jiwan Peeth, Kashi, 1954.

Vinaya Patrika, of Tulsidasa, Geeta Press Gorakhpur (n.d.).

Vishnudharmotra Purana, Gaikwad, Oriental Series No. , Baroda, 1958.

II Secondary Sources

Aggarwala, Vasudeva Sharan, *Prachin Bhartiya Lokdharma,* Jnanodaya Trust, Ahmedabad, 1964.

Aryan, K.C. , *Hanuman in Art and Mythology*, Rekha Prakashan, Delhi, 1975.

"Hanuman Cult", *Illustrated Weekly of India*, Vol. XCVII, March 11, 1976.

Babb, Lawrence A., *The Divine Hierarchy: Popular Hinduism in Central India,* Columbia University Press, New York, 1975.

Bannerjee, J.N., *The Development of Hindu Iconography*, University of Calcutta, Calcutta, 1956.

Ghurye, G.S., *Gods and Men,* Popular Book Depot, Bombay, 1960.

Griffith, R.T.H., *The Ramayana of Valmiki*, Banaras, 1915.

Hazra, R.C., *Studies in the Upa Purana*, Parts I, II, Calcutta 1958, 1963.

Hopkins, E.W., *The Great Epic of India,* New York, 1901.

Jacobi, Harman, *Das Ramayana,* Trans. N.N. Ghoshal, Oriental Institute, Baroda, 1960.

Kalyana, Year 49, Geeta Press, Gorakhpur.

Krishnamchariar, *History of Sanskrit Literature,* Madras, 1937.

Kosambi, D.D., Myth and Reality, Popular Prakashan, Bombay, 1963.

Kulkarni, V.M., "Origin and Development of Rama Story in Jaina Literature", *Journal of Oriental Institute*, Vol. IX, No. 3, March 1960.

Majumdar, Shudha, *The Ramayana,* Orient Longmans, 1958.

Manjula, Sahd, *Valmiki Ramayana aur Sanskrit Natakon Mein Rama,* Vimal Prakashan, Ghaziabad, 1979.

Mishra, Vidya, *Valmiki Ramayana Avam Ramcarita Manas Ka Tulnatamak Adhyana,* Lucknow Vishvadyalaya, Lucknow.

Monier, William, *Sanskrit English Dictionary*, 1899.

Moor, E., *The Hindu Pantheon*, London, 1910.

Muir, J., *Original Sanskrit Texts*, Vol. IV, London, 1873.

Narasimhachar, D.L., "The Jaina Ramayana", *Indian Historical Quarterly,* March 1939.

Navalkara, N.R., *A New Approach to the Ramayana,* Jabalpur, 1957.

O'Flaherty, W.D. *Asceticism and Eroticism in the Mythology of Siva,* Oxford University Press, New York, 1973.

Pargitar, F.E., "Vrsakapi and Hanuman", *Journal of Royal Asiatic Society*, 1911, 1913.

Raghavan, V., *Some Old Lost Rama Plays,* Annamalai University, 1961.

Rai, Govinda Chandra, *Hanuman Ke Devatva Tatha Murti ka Vikas,* Hindi Sahitya Sammelan, Prayag, 1976.

Sen, D.C., *Bengali Ramayana,* University of Calcutta, Calcutta, 1920.

Shah, U.P., " Vrsakapi in Rgveda", *Journal of Oriental Institute,* Vol. 8, September 1968.

Shastri Hari Prasad, *The Ramayana of Valmiki* (trans.), London, 1957.

Thomas, P., *Epics, Myths, and Legends of India*, 9th Edition, Bombay.

The Tribes of Madhya Pradesh, Department of Tribal Welfare, Govt. of Madhya Pradesh, 1964.

Upadhyaya, Ramji, *Adhunik Sanskrit Nataka,* Parts I and II, 1977.

Velankar, H.D., "Hymns to Indra in Mandala 10", *Journal of University of Bombay,* September 1953.

Warder, A.K., *Indian Kavya Literature*, Vol. 1,2,3, Motilal Banarasidas, Delhi, 1972, 1974 and 1977.

Whaling, Frank, *The Rise of the Religious Significance of Rama,* Motilal Banarasidas, Delhi, 1980.

Wolcott, Leonard T., "The Power Dispensing Monkey in North Indian

Folk Religion", *The Journal of Asian Studies*, Vol. 37, November1977.
Winternitz, M., *History of Sanskrit Literature*, Part I, University of Calcutta, Calcutta, 1963.

Appendix

SOURCES OF HANUMAN LEGENDS IN PURĀṆAS, DRAMAS, AND STORIES USED IN THE TEXT

TEXT	AUTHOR	CHRONOLOGY	HIS CHARACTERISTICS AND HIS ROLE IN THE LITERATURE.
Rāmāyaṇa	Vālmīki	Cir. 100-300 A.D.	A loyal and most trustworthy friend of Rāma His role as an ambassador, spy, war strategist.
Paumcariyam	Vimal Suri	Cir. 200-400 A.D.	Birth legends of Hanuman. His exploits.
Pratimā Nāṭaka	Bhāsa	Cir. 300-500 A.D.	Mentioned once after Rama's coronation.
Abhiśeka Nāṭaka	Bhāsa	Cir. 300-500 A.D.	His role as a warrior and ambassador of Rama.
Nara Singh Purāṇa	— —	Cir. 400-500 A.D.	Hanuman's character, his divine birth.
Viṣṇudharmotra Purāṇa	— —	Cir. 500-700 A.D.	Hanuman as Nandī.
Padama Purāṇa (Jain)	Ravisena	Cir. 500-800 A.D.	Hanuman's birth legends and his exploits.

TEXT	AUTHOR	CHRONOLOGY	HIS CHARACTERISTICS AND HIS ROLE IN THE LITERATURE.
Śri Mad Bhāgavata	— —	Cir. 600-700 A.D.	Rāma's devotee.
Bhavisya Purāṇa	— —	Cir. 700 A.D.	Hanuman as *rudrāvatāra* and Rāma's devotee.
Mahāvīra Caritam Nāṭaka	Bhavabhuti	Cir. 700-800 A.D.	Brave and courageous hero called Vṛṣākapi.
Uttara Purāṇa (Jain)	Jinsena Guṇabhadra	Cir. 800-900 A.D.	Hanuman's marriage to 100 girls. Hanuman after attaining Nirvāṇa leaves administration to his sons.
Sakanda Purāṇa	— —	Cir. 800 A.D.	Hanuman as a *rudrāvatāra.*
Narada Purāṇa	— —	Cir. 800-1000 A.D.	Hanuman's character, incarnation of Śiva, his tantric worship.
Anargha Rāghava Nāṭaka	Murari	Cir. 900-1000A.D.	His wonderful feats. His mission to Lankā.
Aścarya Cūḍāmaṇī Nāṭaka	Śaktibhadra	Cir. 900-1000 A.D.	Hanuman as a messenger to Sītā, his role at Sītā's ordeal.

TEXT	AUTHOR	CHRONOLOGY	HIS CHARACTERISTICS AND HIS ROLE IN THE LITERATURE.
Bāla Rāmāyaṇa	Rajśekhra	Cir. 900-1000 A.D.	Hanuman's exploits, scholar of Aṅgavidyā.
Mahābhāgavata Purāṇa	— —	Cir. 1000-1100 A.D.	Incarnation of Śiva.
Mahā-Nāṭaka	Madhusudan Miśrā	Cir. 1000-1400 A.D.	As a *rudrāvatāra.*
Hanumana Nāṭaka	Dāmodara Miśrā	Cir. 1000-1400 A.D.	*Rudrāvatāra* and devotee of Rāma, miraculous deeds.
Prasanna Rāghava Nāṭaka	Jaideva	Cir. 1200 A.D.	His exploits in Lankā.
Saugandhīkāharṃ Nāṭaka	Viśvnātha	Cir. 1291-1322 A.D.	Learned scholar,knowledge of magic charms and devotee of Rāma.
Dutāṅagada Nāṭaka	Subhata	Cir. 1300 A.D.	Rāma's devotee.
Bṛhdharma Purāṇa	— —	Cir. 1300 A.D.	Incarnation of Śiva, extraordinary feats.

TEXT	AUTHOR	CHRONOLOGY	HIS CHARACTERISTICS AND HIS ROLE IN THE LITERATURE.
Ullāgha Rāghava Nāṭaka	Someśvara	Cir. 1300 A.D.	Loyal follower and devotee of Rāma.
Anjana Pavanajava Nāṭaka	Hastimalla	Cir. 1300 A.D.	Hanuman's parentage, his birth legends, marriage and exploits.
Śiva Mahā Purāṇa	— —	Cir. 1400 A.D.	His birth from Śiva, brave hero kills Mahīrāvana.
Ānanda Ramayaṇa	— —	Cir. 1400-1500 A.D.	Hanuman incarnation of Śiva, his worship as a *brahmacāri* folk god.
Brahma Vaīvarta Purāṇa	— —	Cir. 800 A.D. (lost) recast in present from in Cir.1600 A.D. Cir. 1600-1700 A.D.	As a *rudrāṁsa*, his character recast in brief.
Adhyātama Rāmāyaṇa	— —	Cir. 1600-1700 A.D.	As a mediator, brave hero. As a devotee of Rāma, his worship as a folk god.

TEXT	AUTHOR	CHRONOLOGY	HIS CHARACTERISTICS AND HIS ROLE IN THE LITERATURE.
Jānakī Pariṇay	Rambhadra Dikṣita.	Cir. 1700-1800 A.D.	As a mediator, a brave hero.
Adbhuta Darpaṇa	Mahādeva	Cir. 1700 A.D.	As a spy.
Prasanna-Hanuman Nāṭaka	Viśvéswar Dayālu	Cir. 2000 A.D.	His legitimate birth. war hero, exploits.